Confessions
of an
Accidental
Businessman

Other books by James A. Autry

Love and Profit: The Art of Caring Leadership
Life & Work: A Manager's Search for Meaning

POETRY
Nights Under a Tin Roof: Recollections of a Southern Boyhood
Life After Mississippi

Confessions of an Accidental Businessman

It Takes a Lifetime to Find Wisdom

JAMES A. AUTRY

Berrett-Koehler Publishers
San Francisco

Berrett-Koehler Publishers, Inc.
450 Sansome Street, Suite 1200
San Francisco, CA 94111-3320
Tel: 415-288-0260   Fax: 415-362-2512

Ordering Information

Individual sales. Berrett-Koehler publications are available through most
bookstores. They can also be ordered direct from Berrett-Koehler at the
address above.

Quantity sales. Special discounts are available on quantity purchases by corporations, associations, and others. For details, contact the "Special Sales
Department" at the Berrett-Koehler address above.

Orders for college textbook/course adoption use. Please contact Berrett-
Koehler Publishers at the address above.

Orders by U.S. trade bookstores and wholesalers. Please contact Publishers
Group West, 4065 Hollis Street, Box 8843, Emeryville, CA 94662;
510-658-3453; 1-800-788-3123.

Printed in the United States of America

 Printed on acid-free and recycled paper that is composed of
50% recovered fiber, including 10% postconsumer waste.

Library of Congress Cataloging-in-Publication Data
Autry, James A.
    Confessions of an accidental businessman : it takes a lifetime to learn
wisdom / James A. Autry. —1st ed.
        p.   cm.
    isbn 1–57675–003–5 (alk. paper)
    1. Autry, James A.   2. Executives—United States—Biography.
3. Management.   I. Title.
HC102.5.A88A3   1996
658—dc20   96–28186
                                                CIP

First Edition
00 99 98 97 96   10 9 8 7 6 5 4 3 2 1

The poems, "Recessions," "Romantic Revelations," "On Firing A Salesman," and
"Leaving It All Behind," are from **Love and Profit,** copyright 1991 by James A. Autry.
The poem, "Death Message," is from **Life & Work,** copyright 1994 by James A. Autry.
All are by permission of William Morrow & Company, Inc.

Text design by Detta Penna

For Sally . . .

*. . . and in memory of my mother, Ruth,
whose name means, most appropriately,
"compassionate friend."*

*"We have concentrated too
much on the dollar value
of the human and not enough
on the human value
of the dollar."*

—Jonas Salk

Contents

Contents

Preface

Ever since Lee Iacocca wrote his memoirs in the early 1980s, recalling the years at Chrysler, senior business leaders seem drawn to tell us their stories. Sometimes self-published, sometimes professionally published, memoirs or autobiographies of everyone from Thomas Watson to Donald Trump to Sam Walton have lined the bookstore shelves and have turned up regularly on the best-seller lists.

Just think what a great experience it must be to tell the world the story of your business success. You can talk about all the decisions, all the deals done, all the problems overcome, all the challenges met; you can let the readers see the very inner workings of your intellect. It can be an opportunity to share your expertise, to teach the up-and-coming businesspeople how to become successful. It can be, in effect, an act of generosity.

And it can also be an ego trip. After thirty-two years in business, thirty of which were in management and fifteen of which were in senior management with the Meredith Corporation, a Fortune 500 company in Des Moines, Iowa, best known as the publishers of *Better Homes and Gardens*, I know a thing or two about life in the executive suite.

Much of what you have heard is true. Executives do lead a very different life from that of a corporation's other employees. Often, this life is one of privilege, borne of a psychology of entitlement that has become widespread among top corporate officers and is manifest in many superficial ways, such as chauffeured cars, private jets, private rest rooms, private dining rooms, and private hotel suites.

All of this feeds the image you get as a reader of one of those high-profile biographies: extraordinarily impressive people doing extraordinarily impressive things.

But there is another, not-so-superficial and not-so-glamorous side of the executive life. I've been a member of that "club," I've benefitted personally from all its perks and privileges, and I can assure you of this: Most corporate executives are not as impressive as you've come to think (or been led to think). Most of them are pretty regular people who do a very competent job while at the same time suffering the same stuff that plagues us all. They are vulnerable and flawed, fearful of criticism, and terrified of failure. In other words, they are human, but this is not the story we usually hear.

When reading the autobiographies or "authorized" biographies of the superstars, I often find myself wondering what the *real* story was. What were their warts? What mistakes did they make? What were their attitudes twenty years ago, and how did they change and what changed them? I long to hear one of them admit, "I screwed up" or, "I didn't always believe that" or, "I used to be a jerk on this subject." I also long to know about their childhoods, their experiences outside of business, and how those influenced what they did later as business executives.

Is this too much to ask? I think not. The very fact that business biographies and memoirs so often treat business as an entirely separate part of life amply illustrates the problem with business. It is as if all of us in business are conditioned to believe that we must keep business and life separate, that business is some discreet activity apart from the rest of what we do, such as parent our children, engage in life with our spouses, nurture our friendships, and so on.

I believe that the story of a businessperson's life cannot be restricted to those things that make us feel good when we see them on the resume. If the lessons to be taught are framed only in the context of success, then there will be few lessons taught. And the teaching of lessons should be at the heart of storytelling.

I have written two books in which I've tried to offer my thoughts on what an executive's life is like and what qualities I believe should be at the heart of any organization. If you're familiar with either book, you know that they are not typical of the management training literature.

Love and Profit and *Life & Work* are books of essays and poems. In them, I have tried to get underneath all the chest-beating, self-aggrandizing, macho stuff of management and get to the emotion of it in order to examine how deeply the role of manager must engage the very fiber of our lives. I try to explain what I call "caring leadership."

Now, in this book, I continue to explore these subjects but in the context of a memoir of my life in business. Please understand that, although this is biographical, it is not an autobiography. An autobiography requires a great deal of science, in which the emphasis is on a logical progression of events presented in well-researched detail, most often in chronological order.

On the other hand memoirs are, as the word suggests, memories. In this case, they are memories selected because of their impact on my business life, either at the time or later in life. Though I have tried throughout to ensure the accuracy of these recollections, my emphasis has not been on the *facts* of a particular situation or episode. Rather, the emphasis has been on the *truth* and its meaning for me.

A word about how the book is organized: You will notice that the chapters seem to jump around chronologically. That is not strictly true. Chapter One is a chronological overview of my life in business. Chapter Two is an almost chronological overview of my life in management. Chapter Three is the first of the "thematic" chapters, which indeed transcend time and show how a certain theme occurred throughout my career. From that point on, the chapters alternate between a strictly chronological approach (Chapter Four is the first of those) and a thematic approach. For example, if you wanted to proceed strictly chronologically, you'd jump from Chapter Four to Chapter Six to Chapter Eight, and so on.

Another unusual element in the arrangement of this book is the occasional insertion of poetry within chapters and between chapters. In speaking to business groups, it frequently has been my poetry that has most inspired, impressed, and instructed managers at all levels. "Instructed" may seem an unusual function for a poem, but it has been through poetry that I have tried to give voice to, and honor, the emotions we feel about our work, and to suggest that the most important connections we have to our work and to one another are emotional. Just as this book has not been all about the work lessons I've learned on the job itself, but about the interconnection of lessons learned throughout life, these poems are not focused specifically on the world of work.

I realize I am asking a lot of you, the reader, but I hope you will find this arrangement effective and not just confusing.

I also hope that, if you are contemplating management as a career, these writings will lead you to pay attention, to be aware, to always look for the connections between all your experiences in life. If you already are well into your career or even at the end of it, I hope you will be inspired to examine themes and memories thoughout your own life to explore how they have influenced your business journey and to find, as I have, enormous satisfaction in the process.

James A. Autry
Des Moines, Iowa
June 1996

Acknowledgments

Three years ago, on the Saturday night before my wife Sally and I were to leave for a vacation in France, she said to me, "Jim, may I ask a special favor of you?"

"Of course," I answered.

"Would you consider not taking your computer on this vacation with us?" She continued, "You have been writing a book on every vacation we've had since we were married, and I would appreciate it if you could leave it behind one time."

"No problem," I assured her, "I don't really need to start on the new book right now anyway."

So I left the computer in my office and took only a yellow legal pad and a few pencils, thinking I might be able to dabble with some poetry along the way.

The next week, we set off with our friends, Wes Graham and Virginia Traxler. After the excitement settled and we'd had a little champagne and some dinner and were high above the dark Atlantic, I said to Sally, "You know I've been thinking about writing my business memoirs instead of another book of essays and poetry about business."

"Sounds like a good idea," she said. "Maybe you need a new format."

After a pause I said, "Whenever I think about how to begin the story of my life in business, my mind always goes back to the time my father left our home in Memphis and did not return. What do you make of that, Honey?"

I will never forget the moment. Sally looked at me, I think with deep compassion, and then she said softly, "I think I make the first sentence of it."

I reached up to the seat pocket in front of me, took out the yellow pad, and began to write that sentence. Sally smiled and went to sleep, and I wrote for three hours.

Thank you once again, Sally. I would have felt fully blessed with you as wife and friend and spiritual companion; that you are also muse is far more than I bargained for.

Not every publisher is interested in an autobiographical business book, or memoir; in fact, some publishers are downright scared to take the risk. So I send a special note of appreciation to Steve Piersanti and his wonderful team at Berrett-Koehler Publishers, who seem to have the gift of seeing the good in manuscripts—as well as in people.

I want to thank my agent, Rafe Sagalyn, who not only persevered with this manuscript but who also made very helpful suggestions for rewrites and revisions.

Thanks also to the Rev. Ms. Patricia de Jong for reading and critiquing the chapter on "witnessing," and to my associate, Deb McCarroll, for everything that she does to conserve my time and energy.

I could not begin to acknowledge all the friends and colleagues with whom I have been so abundantly blessed. In a way, this book is a list of acknowledgments of those who have contributed to my life and to my search for understanding, or wisdom. The search continues, of course, and so do the friendships.

Trying to Reach Everyone's Story

Everyone has a story. The poet William Stafford once said that the writer's job is to dig so deep into his own story that he reaches everyone's story. It's a difficult job because, in truth, all of us have many stories within our big one.

The big story is life itself. We are men or women, lovers and friends, spouses and parents, teachers and students, workers and bosses, colleagues and rivals. We shape events and we are shaped by events. We celebrate and grieve, struggle and prevail, succeed and fail.

Everything we do is a story in itself, part of a larger story, and part of a yet even larger story. So often, as young people, we feel we must somehow learn about life so we then can go out and live life. This is the stuff of popular fiction, with scenes of a young man or woman getting on the bus or hopping a freight train or signing on with the circus, saying something like, "I want to get out of this place and go where I can learn about life."

Later, we discover that *we learn everything there is to learn about life from living our own stories.* That discovery is the first step of a lifetime journey toward wisdom, a search that never ends because, indeed, it takes a full lifetime to find wisdom.

Within my own story, my life in business is the dominant theme, yet I know it does not stand as a self-contained narrative, disconnected from the events and relationships that shaped and influenced me throughout life. Thus I cannot tell it as a separate story. To do so would be to misrepresent and distort its truth.

I know that most business memoirs and biographies tend to compartmentalize business experiences within their own context, reducing personal references and activities to mere sidebars on the main story. But I also recognize that people and circumstances outside our professional world have a profound influence on our attitudes and actions in business.

For instance, one of my CEO friends grew up wealthy. His attitude regarding compensation and benefits for his employees is very different from another CEO friend who grew up in a working-class family. I submit that the manager whose father or mother was a high-level executive brings a whole different mind-set to management than does the manager whose father or mother was an assembly-line union worker. And no amount of sophisticated business education can completely eliminate or neutralize those attitudes.

Sometimes a dramatic experience in an executive's life intrudes to bring about a workplace change of significance. I know a CEO who became addicted to alcohol. He thought he was doing a great job and that his drinking did not impair his ability to perform. He did not drink during working hours, he said, so there was no impact on his work.

Only later, through his involvement with a twelve-step program, did he realize that not only had his drinking affected both his personal and professional lives but that his recovery could affect those as well. His twelve-step work and his "membership" in the recovery group made him understand that all groups, all communities—including his employee group—are made up of flawed people, and that those flaws can be overcome. As a result of this realization, he has changed the entire atmosphere in his company, creating an environment of support instead of fear. This change has produced record revenues and profits. Now, could his business success story be told without also telling of his long and quiet and largely internal struggle to recover?

Though I could not have articulated it this way at the time, I know that much of my imperative toward creating a workplace environment of caring management was due to the uncaring treatment that my mother received as a low-level worker and that I received in the first decade of my working life.

Of course, I also believed—and believe—that a supportive environment fulfills powerful business purposes of finding and keeping good people and making them more productive. But I would not swear which of those beliefs and conditionings were most instrumental in the evolution of my leadership philosophies and techniques over the years.

Could it be that a sensitivity toward the front line workers helped me become as successful as I did? I believe so, just as I believe that this sensitivity made me too tolerant from time to time, too willing to overlook mistakes and lesser performance. It cut both ways. On balance, however, my successes surely had their beginning not when I took on the mantle of corporate executive but when I was a newspaper carrier, perhaps, or construction worker, or copy boy, or farmhand, or something back there years ago when my whole future seemed headed toward wages and not salary, toward labor and not management, toward a life of rented apartments, used cars, and "time payments."

I have had to ask tough questions about my attitudes

toward business and how they changed. How did I go from being one of society's "have nots," disappointed and angry about what others had and I didn't, to an income in the top one percent of U.S. households? How did I go from believing that business, its political influence, its manipulation of our wants and desires, and its greed were central to the country's problems, to knowing that business can be a reliable and enduring source of social good? How did I stop thinking of "bosses" as people with power over me and people at whose whims I succeeded or failed, to thinking of management as a helping profession that could be dedicated to assuring that people who want to succeed have all the resources and support they need to succeed?

The answers to those questions and others are at the heart of the story I tell on these pages. Although, by its nature, this is not a management how-to book, I nonetheless have felt it imperative to ensure that there are valuable lessons of leadership and management in every chapter—lessons that cannot be dismissed as irrelevant to the way things are done today. I know that with today's pressures of downsizing, of demands for ever-increasing productivity, of unprecedented competitiveness, there is the temptation to invalidate everything that happened in business during the past decade.

But good leadership transcends time and knows no chronological barriers, because good leadership is not about *doing*. It is about *being* and it is about creating the context for an organization, creating how the organization is to *be*, no matter what is to be done.

Since 1992, after taking early retirement so that I could write, I have found myself lecturing a great deal, consulting a bit, and serving on boards of directors. My purpose, in all these roles, is to help break down the barriers between employees and bosses, between wage earners and salary earners, between labor and management. Regardless of the particular pressures a company and its people may be under these days, I have found that counterproductive barriers still are most easily overcome in an atmosphere of openness, honesty, and trust.

This book is very much about overcoming barriers and about learning how to *be* in life and in business, and my abiding purposes in writing it have been:

- First, to tell my story in a way that I hope will touch many people's stories by demonstrating how it can look and feel to strive toward a good business life.

- If you are a manager, to help you recognize that you *aready know* in the most fundamental sense how to be a manager, that the source of that knowledge comes not from formal business training but from deep within yourself, and to encourage you to manage from that true self, even if you occasionally find it in conflict with "the way things are done."

- To lead you, as a manager, to think of your organization as a community of work and, in turn, to support your employees in thinking of it that way and participating in it.

- To help you overcome any discomfort you may feel about spirituality and work, and to affirm that indeed there is something ineffable that binds people in a common endeavor, a spirit of work that is very powerful when you recognize and nurture it.

- To be open about the ethical dilemmas and moral conflicts I faced and to be honest about my motives, my frailties, and my mistakes, thus to reassure you that everyone makes mistakes, that you don't have to be defined by your mistakes, and that with courage you can learn and grow from every one of them.

- And finally, to help you pay attention to all of life's experiences, particularly your relationships, and to recognize and examine how all of them are connected—whether those experiences are from childhood or college or mid-career, whether those relationships are with a friend, a lover, a spouse, a parent, a child, a colleague, a customer, a vendor, a manager, or an employee—*then to look inside your deepest self as the most dependable guide to being the best person you can be, wherever you are and whatever you do.*

✑ Man of the House

The first scar came when the boy jumped a barbed wire fence
on the way to school.

When the wire tore into the flesh of his calf it was not the pain
that made him cry but the anger that this would not have
happened if his mother had let him walk the drainage ditch
to school.

"If there's a flood, you will drown," she had said which was
dumb as hell since it wasn't about to rain but she had been
crying again so he had not argued.

His third grade teacher sent him home because he was tracking
blood and she said he needed stitches. She knew his
mother would be looking for a job but his teacher sent
him home anyway, his shoe squishing blood at every step.

The banty rooster was gone, and the hens, two or three days,
so he was not all that surprised when Mickey did not come
at his whistle. Still, he was too heartbroken not to cry.

His pants were ruined maybe, torn, bloody, but he put them
in the tub to soak then he washed his leg, poured coal oil
on a rag and pressed it onto the gash.

Damn it hurt.

The boy wondered why he had miscalculated, had missed
the jump, but he had known as he left the ground that he
would not be high enough. He remembered thinking, that
instant in the air, he should have just walked the ditch.

But he was trying to be a man for his mother as she had told
him he would now have to be even though he knew she
still wanted him to be a child.

He had liked the idea of being the man of the house but after
three weeks it was not working out that way.

The man of the house would have known about the bantys and
would not have let them be taken away, and the man of the
house would have his dog to call when he came home.

The boy did not understand all that had happened but he knew
that many things were happening without his knowing why.
He knew he had not seen his father since the night they were
going on a camping trip, were walking out the driveway to
where his father had said the car was parked and loaded,
and his mother came screaming, "No you don't, no you
don't. You're not taking him with you."
The boy had looked out to the street where the car sat idling.
He wanted to go but his mother, pushing past his father,
grabbed his hand and pulled him back. His father
grabbed the other hand, and they stood that way for a
while, his mother crying, his father saying, "Come on, son,
don't you want to go camping with Dad?" Then his mother
saying, "You are not taking him from this house. I know
what you're planning to do. For God's sake, leave me
somebody who loves me." She was sobbing.
The boy felt his father's hand slip away like someone falling.
Then the car was leaving and his father was gone.
The boy knew he could not take his father's place in this house.
He could not even try.
Pulling the blood and coal oil soaked rag from his leg and tying
a towel around it, he decided that all he could do now was
try not to cry.
Later he told his mother it was her fault he had torn his leg.
She seemed to accept this verdict and he could tell she
was choking on her tears again.
The next day, and every day after that, without asking anyone,
he walked the drainage ditch to school.
As for the torn leg it healed finally, without stitches,
and that scar is hardly visible today.

Chapter One

From Government Housing to Executive Suite

Whenever I think about how to begin this story of my life in business, my mind always goes back to the time my father left our home in Memphis and did not return.

My mother, who had studied art at an all-girls' Baptist college in Mississippi, was not prepared to support a six year-old son and herself. She tried to teach art, but there was no money in it. After a lack of income drove us to move from our nice neighborhood to Lamar Terrace, a federal government housing project, I learned many lessons about life, about power, about class and status—and about what people might do for no reason at all and how that could make me feel. On the first day at the Terrace, my mother encouraged me to go out on the big playground and fly my kite. A tough-looking little kid named Louie Bookout, on a dare from bigger boys, walked up, grabbed my kite string, snapped it, then said in tough-guy fashion of the day, "Wanna make something of it?" I managed not to cry, but I was so scared I broke out in hives.

In those days, just as World War II was beginning, Mother went from one job to another, learning a lot of lessons she had never even dreamed of about life, about power, about class and status, about men who accosted her with no provocation at all—one of them asking her once in front of me and before I knew what it meant if she would like a bedfellow—and about bosses who worked her hard and paid her poorly.

After working in five-and-dime retail sales and briefly on a "war plant" assembly line, she got a job with Memphis Light, Gas, and Water Company, working "in an office," a distinction that seemed to mean a lot to her. A few years later, Mother made a great breakthrough when she studied and learned to use a comptometer machine, which for its day was a super adding machine/calculator, thus improving her status and her pay. I remember being proud and impressed when, at church, she told people she was a comptometer operator, pronouncing "comptometer" musically as if it were a foreign word.

"What do you do at the Light Company, Ruth?" people would ask, the women being somewhat suspicious of any woman who worked outside the home.

"I'm a comptometer operator," she would answer, her voice rising in the middle of the word, at the "tom" syllable, imbuing it, I'm sure she thought, with special and substantial meaning.

I think now how pathetic it was and must have seemed to the church businessmen who knew about such menial things.

But I did not know about business, or businessmen, in those days. I had never thought about business as such; I did not understand it even objectively, so there was no basis whatsoever for grasping its abstractions. To my mind, business had the stuff I wanted, and Mother and I did not have the money to buy it.

The local grocery store was a Weona store run by a short Italian-American man and his family. They always seemed nice enough until the day the man intercepted Mother and me at the door and said we could not buy anything more until the bill was paid.

I thought we should pay the bill and never go back, but it was the only place we could buy groceries on credit, so I could find my only satisfaction in fantasizing how someday I would have enough money to buy the store, then as the man watched, I'd burn it to the ground. It was a time when proprietors loved the businesses into which they had put their lives, so it never occurred to me that, having sold his store, the man might not care what I did with it. In my dream, he would plead with me not to torch the place where he had worked so hard and where, in rooms above the store, he had raised his family.

That experience—of being denied credit, of seeing my mother's tearful embarrassment, of feeling hostage to someone's control over what I could buy and even over what I could eat—stays with me still, and I believe it helped me be more careful in my position as a boss who had great influence over people's incomes, their futures, their ability to achieve their dreams.

My naive understanding of business was not helped by my friend Jack Davis, whose father owned a drug store. Jack would, whenever he wished, it seemed to me, take money from any cash register in the place—money with which he was always generous with his friends.

Like most kids of that era, I had not even the most remote notion of how a retail store worked. I just assumed that all the money in the cash register belonged to Jack's father.

Years later, I learned the pressures of the margin squeeze during which all that money in the cash register—the revenue—looks pretty good until the costs of doing business are paid. Then, looking back, I understood how Mr. Davis must have felt when he discovered that son Jack was giving the profits to his little friends to go to the Saturday matinee and buy popcorn and Walnettos and Raisinettes.

My journey to the understanding of business began, as

it still does for many young people, as a newspaper carrier. Mine was the least desirable route in the district, serving an economically mixed neighborhood, from Lamar Terrace to the mansions on Central to the poor white shanties along the railroad tracks.

Some boys learn about the joy of profit from their paper routes, I suppose, but I learned mostly about slow pays and bad pays and no pays, and that there was often little correlation between those customers who could pay, the ones in the mansions on Linden, and those who would pay. Some of my best payers lived in the poor white shotgun houses along the tracks. All they wanted was the paper on the porch early before they went to work at whatever hard labor jobs they held, and they paid on Friday evenings, on schedule. Some of the mansion people paid on time, but many were awfully quick to say, "I don't have thirty-five cents right now; come back tomorrow," then climb into a Packard or a Cord or some other car no one else drove.

Or they might say, "Have change for a twenty?" My route was one hundred papers, thirty-five cents a week. Total: thirty-five dollars, if everyone paid. My take was about five dollars a week, if everyone paid. I would *never* have change for a twenty. "Pay you next week," they'd say.

I learned about bosses—the route managers—who pressed constantly to do more, to "build your route," and so on, but would never help with a customer who would not pay or who had a bad dog.

In other words, all that stuff about learning to be your own businessman was lost on me. I dreamed of the day I'd be sixteen and able to get a job, go do it, and collect my wages. At that time I believe I was, by nature, *Labor*.

In high school, I became a copy boy for the Associated Press, thus launching my journalism career. Clearly, I was not headed for the businessman's life. To the contrary, the more I worked as a low-level employee, the more I came to resent the bosses who, it seemed to me for no reason at all, held such sway over my life. They scheduled my hours, determined my pay, watched me as I worked, and clocked me in and out to the minute, for arrival and departure, for lunch or dinner breaks, or for coffee breaks.

Of course I did not even understand why there were coffee breaks or why lunch periods were set for cerain periods of time. At one point early in the copy boy job, I made it my practice to eat and come right back to work, often cutting my lunch break in half. It seemed silly to let the copy on the teletype machines pile up while I stood around with nothing else to do but file it. So I would file it as usual.

After a couple of weeks, a co-worker, a senior teletype operator named Harrell Allen, took me aside. "Listen," he said, "I know you want to do a good job, but you can't give these people more time than they pay for. You make it hard on everybody. The union fought for these hours and you have to abide by them even if you don't belong to the union."

I stammered that I did not understand the rules and that I was just trying to save myself more work later on by coming back a little early. "Don't do it," he said.

Some time later, working the same shift with Harrell, I learned that he was a staunch unionist, something that meant as little to me as did the notion of businessman.

"If you're union, they can't jack you," he would say. One late evening when news was slow, he told me his vision: "Some day all of us will be organized in the same union, telephone operators, Western Union operators, teletype operators, all the people who keep the communications going in this country. Then, by God, when we speak they'll have to listen, they'll have to give us what we deserve or we'll shut down all the communicaton in this country."

I was astonished at the thought of it, but I liked it. That's right, I thought. They (whoever they were) would have to give us what we deserve. I went through the motions of becoming a member of the Commercial Telegraphers Union, though I believe I was too young and never became a member. It was my first taste of taking sides in the great management-labor conflict, which reached such dramatic heights after World War II.

When I headed for college in 1951 to study journalism, I learned that there even was a union for journalists, presumably to protect them from rapacious publishers. Much later, when I became a business manager, this struck me as a clear violation of journalistic objectivity that journalists supposedly hold so sacred.

But journalism school was no place to think about such weighty things, just as it is no place to learn about business. In fact, most journalism professors are so concerned about teaching their graduates the techniques of ferreting out corruption in high places that the notion of journalism as business never makes it past a few minor courses on weekly newspaper management and perhaps a survey course or two on the corporation and society (or some such title). Of course, there are the students who major in public relations or advertising, courses included in most schools of "mass communication" as they now like to be called, but those students are not "real" journalism students, if you know what I mean. And the "real" journalism professors, if you know what I mean, don't have a very high regard for those students.

So I did not learn about business in college. Instead, I learned to look for corruption in high places and how to manage a weekly newspaper. I made a college career as a crusading reporter and editor with the student newspaper. Lord, I was impressed with my recognition and awards. If I could just get a job on a big metropolitan daily newspaper, there clearly was a Pulitzer Prize in my future.

However, time changes expectations, so I was shocked when, after four years of flying jet fighters in the U.S. Air Force—a not unglamorous job at a pretty good salary including flying pay—the only job I could find in civilian life was as editor of a weekly newspaper in Humboldt, Tennessee, for fifty dollars a week. And I was expected to sell office supplies in the front office, help set type and make up the forms for the old flatbed press, and—God help me—*sell advertising* to the local merchants. The local people, particularly the businesspeople, thought of the newspaper as their own, and by their definition the paper was to be a positive community booster, not a detractor. So my stories about local speeders and the declined state of the airport did not help my advertising sales. It was my first lesson in the old business concept of reciprocity.

As for corruption in high places, there weren't even any high places, and the corruption, as in many small towns, was so ingrained no one there recognized it as corruption.

I was rescued from that job in 1960 by an offer from *Better Homes and Gardens* in Des Moines, Iowa, to become Copy Editor, the lowest position on the editorial staff.

In my first week on the job, it became clear to me that I had no notion what I was supposed to do and, apart from some basic writing and editing skills, was manifestly unqualified to be a magazine editor. My only hope was that no one else had figured it out yet.

It was to be many years before "mentoring" made its way into the business lexicon, and although I'm sure it went on in some form back then, I was simply too scared to ask my superiors for help. I thought I was supposed to know already what to do. And I damned well would never ask peers for assistance, an act that would quickly communicate my ignorance and incompetence to those with whom I thought I should compete to get ahead. As a fighter pilot, I had been taught to always "check six o'clock"—meaning to always make sure there was no enemy on my tail where he could easily shoot me down—so I was not going to let a peer get on my tail. After all, in my new civilian life, who knew who the enemies were?

By that paranoid reasoning, the only option left to me was a self-education process in which I gave myself the equivalent of an advanced degree in magazine journalism which, when you're talking about such service journals as *Better*

Homes and Gardens, does not involve corruption in high places.

The next step in my career was to a "management" position, Managing Editor, in 1962. I was even less qualified for this job, and once again, fearing to look ignorant or foolish, I began a self-education process about management. I knew that being a manager was different from being an Operations Officer or a Squadron Commander but I was not sure how. I read books, attended lectures, and watched other managers. There seemed no relationship between the books and lectures and what the managers actually did.

People seemed to like working for some bosses and to hate working for others, and there seemed no correlation between the quantity and quality of work produced and the boss' popularity or lack of it. I know now that I was learning something about what not to do, how not to manage, although it took years to gain the experience and maturity and courage to do what should be done. I don't believe I was even close to it by the time I resigned as Managing Editor in 1966.

I was offered what I thought to be an opportunity back in "grassroots journalism." However, after a couple of years as editor and publisher of *New Orleans Magazine*—a job that seemed more like running a small retail business than running a magazine, and a job that taught me the hard way a great deal about business fundamentals—I took the first opportunity to return to Meredith as Editorial Director of a newly comprised department, Special Interest Publications.

This turned out to be one of my most rewarding and instructive management experiences. I was put in charge of a group of editors and designers who were producing several annual publications. My charge was to increase the number of existing publications, to start new ones, and to explore other publishing business opportunities.

The people were not only creative and innovative, they were very hard workers who had received little recognition and relatively low pay as the department had been previously organized. My job turned out to be little more than to set some goals, take away the constraints, provide some rewards, and get out of the way. Now we call it "empowerment," but then I thought of it as taking off the harnesses and letting them run. In eighteen months, we went from six publications to eighteen and started a whole new group that became a major profit center.

It was fun, but at the time I did not think it took any particular skill as a manager. I worked hard but was surprised every time I was promoted. That I became the chief editorial person in Meredith Corporation, publishers of *Better Homes and Gardens*, then President of its Magazine Group until I took early retirement in 1992, seemed to me at each step along the way a series of surprising decisions by my bosses followed by a lot of scrambling and self-education, though I finally learned to ask for help and advice from the people whose leadership I admired.

Looking back at my career and looking now at other managers moving up in their organizations, I understand the overall lesson: We frequently underestimate ourselves, we frequently know more than we think we do, and our instincts and judgment are more reliable than we think.

To summarize my career since early retirement—but at the risk of sounding like those self-aggrandizing superstars I mentioned in the introduction—I have now authored successful books on management, which have been reprinted in five languages, which have been anthologized in several collections, and which are on the reading lists of business schools at several universities. I have been invited to countless conferences as speaker and workshop leader, have received awards for my "influence on executive thinking," and am engaged regularly as a consultant both here and abroad. I am on the Boards of Directors of two companies and chair the Board of Advisors of another.

I have not been a journalist in many years. I do not have,

and will not get, a Pulitzer Prize. I am, without question and beyond debate, a businessman. Yet all I had wanted to do was get a job as a newspaperman and make fifty dollars a week.

No wonder I think of myself as an accidental businessman.

❧ Reminiscence at Toul

Thirty years ago
on New Year's eve
drunk on French champagne
we shot bottle rockets
from the windows
of Hank and Willi's
rented chateau overlooking Nancy.

It sounds so worldly
which is how we wanted to think of ourselves,
but Lord, we were just children,
sent by the government to fly airplanes
and to save western Europe
from World War III.

We thought we had all the important things
still left to do
and were just playing at importance
for the time being.
It never occurred to us,
living in our community of friends,
having first babies,
seeing husbands die,
helping young widows pack to go home,
that we had already started the important things.
What could we have been thinking,
or perhaps it's how could we have known
that times get no better,
that important things come without background music,
that life is largely a matter of paying attention.

Chapter Two

Learning About Management and Leadership the Hard Way

Whenever I think about how to begin this story of my life in management, my mind always goes back to the time I was a jet fighter pilot during the Cold War in Europe. It was a dream time in many ways, and much of it seem far removed from any sense of organization or structure. On the face of it, there seemed not much I could have learned about management and leadership. That turned out not to be true.

An air force fighter squadron was to me, and to many of us I suspect, more of a combination family-community-home than it was an organization. (I realize now that this is true also of many companies, regardless of their products or organizational structure.)

After a rough and rolling Atlantic crossing on an aging troop ship and an all-night, low-priority troop train ride across Germany and into France, my three-month-pregnant wife, Jackie, and I arrived in Chaumont, France, expecting to be welcomed by representatives from the base. There was no one to meet us, and our hotel reservation had been botched. Another couple—a sergeant and his wife—arrived as we did, but the Hotel de France had only one available room.

As a lieutenant, I outranked the sergeant and could simply have taken the room—indeed, he assumed I would—but that didn't seem fair to me. So, over his protest, I suggested we flip a coin. We did, he won. What I failed to understand was that, in the interest of fair treatment, I violated his expectations of how things should be. Whereas at the time I thought he would consider me a thoughtful and fair officer, I realized later that he probably just thought I had a lot to learn about being an officer.

(He was right, and as a corporate manager, I learned over the years that regardless of how noble my motives might be or how much I felt employees would benefit from a particular policy or action, anything that violates employees' perceptions of the "way things are done" must be accompanied by a *lot* of education and training.)

The Hotel de France arranged a room at the Hotel de Gare, which I learned later was generally known as a local house of ill-repute.

My wife and I literally huddled in a cold room all night listening to angry shouts and raucous laughter, both in a language we did not understand. According to all my social conditioning, I was to be the good provider and strong protector in the family, and here I had led my wife to a strange land where we put a chair against the door of our room in this hotel whorehouse to protect us from who knew what.

Things changed the next day, and we were welcomed into a community of support that can be understood only by those who have been stationed on a small military base in a foreign country in those years barely a decade after the end of World War II.

I think now of all the high school and college kids of my acquaintance who regularly spend a summer or a semester with a family in another land, who travel effortlessly and speak other languages effortlessly, and I smile to think how utterly unprepared I was for the world.

I had gone from the comfort of a campus one year into what seemed an almost alien life the next. Pilot training was not just the learning of a new skill but a transition of context, a dramatic shift from a world in which my decisions may have seemed important at the time but really were trivial, to a world in which miscalculation, misjudgment, ineptness or simply the failure to carry one's load were often fatal.

The move from a campus in Mississippi to an isolated air base in France was more than a change in geography; it was a change in how I related to the world, and it was the beginning of a change in how I would come to understand the world.

Still, in the air force experiences, the preeminence of my work as the focal point of my life exposed me to lessons of management I was to reflect on for many years.

Theory Versus Reality

Of course, as an officer, I had done all the obligatory classroom study of organization and structure, command and span of control, regulations, policies, procedures, and so on, but like most young officers (and managers), I was to learn that organizations operate with two often-separate mind-sets.

One is concerned with theory and structure, with how things are done—or to put it another way, with doing things right. The other is concerned with direct operations, with motivating people to get things done effectively, and with ensuring that the right things get done. In the air force, the theory and structure managers concentrate on such things as filling in the boxes that indicate that all the proper missions have been flown and that all the pilots have done their quota of flying hours in every category. The direct operations managers, if successful, become leaders who maintain enthusiasm in the face of a very dangerous job, who keep morale high and commitment strong, and who focus on the pilots' readiness rather than on the bureaucratic measurements of that readiness. The latter managers understand the truth of that old military saying, "You can't *manage* people into dying for their country; you must lead them."

My squadron commander, his executive officer, and my flight leaders were direct operations managers. Watching them work with the squadron pilots, I came to believe—as many young pilots do—that those of us flying the airplanes were supposed to be immune to all the rules by which the "non-rated" officers (the "ground-pounders," the "beetle crunchers"—in other words, the wing headquarters bureaucrats who did not fly) had to perform their less-than-important jobs.

(It was stunning, years later, to realize that salespeople of a company, as primary revenue generators, often take on this "pilot" role and express much frustration with the "corporate headquarters types" who are always sending memos, writing policies, and hassling everyone about their expense reports.)

Despite my buck pilot arrogance, I did learn some lessons about leadership and management, about authority and responsibility and delegation, about team-building and increasing productivity, about support and compassion, and about the withholding of support and compassion.

While concerning myself principally with the macho jock life of the fighter pilot, many lessons of what to do and what not to do still managed to make their way into my consciousness, and I found myself calling on many of these lessons during my life in business management.

That this could be true begins with the understanding that most companies are organized exactly the way the military is. It is for good reason that we refer to the "command/control" model of management. The military was first, not the other way around. And most managers are taught, or learn somehow, that their jobs are to enforce the rules of the organization and to achieve conformity to those rules. Often, the enforcement of the rules is hard on the human spirit, yet it is the human spirit—I also learned in the air force—that is the force underpinning every human achievement.

How to Recognize a Leader

There are managers, of course, who somehow are able to unleash the power of the human spirit by using the organization's rules and policies and procedures ("regulations") to *enable* people rather than to restrict them. Those managers are the ones we come to call "leaders."

My first squadron commander was a leader, and I still think of him that way, although I was to learn firsthand that his leadership had its limits. He was Major Otto C. Kemp. We had what I would now recognize as a covenant with Major Kemp: He would keep the command/control administration brass ("wing weenies," we called them) away so that we could maintain an open, informal atmosphere and could perform our mission and make him look good in the process. This management style can work well for any manager who knows he or she is evaluated on *results*, not *style*.

The wing commander and his staff always, it seemed to me, looked askance at Major Kemp and his troops when we gathered at the Officers' Club to drink and sing and tell stories. At some point in the evening, one of our flight leaders would offer what came to be our squadron cheer, aimed at Major Kemp:

> Leader: "Otto spelled backwards is . . . "
> Group: "Otto!"
> Leader: "Otto spelled inside out is. . . . "
> Group: "Too-o-o-oot!"

This apparent evidence of "fraternization" between superior and subordinates would make other senior officers grimace. The wing commander was quoted once as having said, "Kemp makes the mistake of trying to be too much one of the troops."

Our reaction was that the wing commander was full of shit.

Not very different from the reaction I now have to managers who feel they must remain aloof and not "get too close" to their employees.

On the other hand, I once had a boss who was so much "one of the troops" that he considered it a lack of personal loyalty if an employee chose not to join the group for an after-work drink or participate in the inevitable weekend party.

That also has to do with what I call leadership. The leader must create loyalty to the enterprise, the mission, and to the team—not personally to the boss.

The Rights of the Team Versus the Rights of the Individual

This is a tough balancing act, and one I struggled with. Sometimes the leader must interpret positively the intentions and direction of the institution itself; at other times, the leader must mitigate the excesses of the institution. It was in this regard that Major Kemp failed me and at the same time demonstrated that it is possible *to be a good team leader but to focus so much on the needs of the team that you ignore, and do injury to, the individuals on the team.*

It was a spring day in 1957 and I had just returned from a bombing mission on the practice range in the desert southwest of Tripoli, Libya. After shutting down my F-100 and debriefing the mission with my flight leader, I returned to the barracks where I knew the beers would soon be popped and the "hangar flying" would begin.

A friend, Captain Goetz, was reading a letter from his wife who, along with all our wives, remained at our home base in Chaumont while we made our regular trips to North Africa for gunnery practice.

Confessions of an Accidental Businessman

"Hey, Jim," he said, "Did you know your wife is back in the hospital?"

I did not know. Jackie had given birth to our first son only a couple of weeks earlier. In fact, I had been sent to Africa when Jimmy was only six days old. It had bothered me that my wife would be alone in a house trailer on a small base in a foreign country with a six-day-old infant, her first, and I would be 1,500 miles away, with no telephones nor with any other way to communicate quickly except in an extreme emergency. Our planes flying back and forth carried letters, so delivery was sporadic. The only comfort was in knowing that the wives took care of one another during these times of separation.

It turned out that Jackie had been in the hospital for several days before Marge Goetz's letter arrived in Tripoli telling her husband that Jackie had suffered post-partum depression and was unable to care for the baby and had to be hospitalized.

Apparently my superior officers, including Major Kemp, had judged this not to be enough of an emergency to recall me from Africa and, in fact, had consciously chosen to let me go ahead and qualify on our new weapons system before even informing me of my wife's illness.

Soon after that episode, I made the decision not to pursue a career as an air force officer. Not that this episode was the only deciding factor, but I did know that I did not want to have my personal life held hostage to the vagaries of "superior officers" and their judgments about what would be in my best interest.

Rank and Power Come in Many Guises

I figured that, in civilian life working for a company, there would be more humanity and more regard for the individual. I was sure that serious family problems would always be accommodated and would take precedent over the considerations of getting the job done.

This of course only demonstrates how naive I still was about business in 1959.

I returned to a world in which companies concerned themselves not only with how employees dressed but with how their spouses (mostly wives at that time) dressed, some companies going so far as to publish guidebooks of social dress and behavior for various occasions.

I once was told by a boss to have a discussion with one of my fellow employees about his tendency to wear argyle socks instead of over-the-calf dark socks. It was one of the most embarrassing conversations I ever had as a new manager, and my colleague never forgot it because some twenty-five years later when I retired, he gave me a pair of argyle socks.

The sixties were a time when employees were expected to suspend their own personal and family needs for the good of the company, and careers often depended on the willingness to move anywhere, anytime, and back again. People joked that IBM stood for "I been moved." And there were other, less printable, jokes.

It was a time also when companies made great show of being clubs or families. At the Meredith Publishing Company (later Meredith Corporation), we were referred to as "members." The all-company memos would be addressed to "All Meredith Members." No one seemed to question what we might be members of. During my first week at Meredith, there was a welcoming coffee in the cafeteria for new employees. I was impressed by the congeniality and hospitality of it all. My military duty had led me to address men of senior rank as "sir," so naturally when I first was introduced to the high-ranking civilian bosses at the coffee, I called them "sir." The chairman of the board at the time said, "Damn it, Jim, call me Fred."

"Wow," I thought, what a difference from the military. It seemed so egalitarian, but after only a few months, I discovered that there were many subtle ways to express status and there were many subtle ways to convey submission to authority without saying "sir" or saluting.

Still, it was a heady feeling being part of the staff of a national magazine, *Better Homes and Gardens*, and I couldn't have been more impressed by my good fortune, despite the fact that I was earning considerably less salary than as an air force pilot. Once, when remarking on how happy I was to be on the staff, a man who was to become a close friend, Red Seney, said, "If you feel that good here at headquarters, just wait until you start traveling and learn the 50-mile rule." He explained that, in Des Moines, we were all considered Meredith employees, but when the airliner passed over an imaginary 50-mile line, we became editors of *Better Homes and Gardens*; and in other cities, where people knew and loved the magazine but had never heard of the company, we were treated with great respect.

As it turned out, that imaginary transformation from Meredith employee to national magazine editor was important for morale and self-esteem. People at the top of the company signaled in many different ways their regard for the editorial staff as just so many employees. The chairman was quoted, perhaps inaccurately, as having said he could hire a bunch of Drake University journalism students to put out the magazine if he had to. Because there was a rumor that the American Newspaper Guild was going to approach our writers about joining, we interpreted the chairman's comment as a veiled threat about any talk of unionization. He was also quoted as having said, while leading a tour of visiting business associates past the graphic design department, "This is where we keep the artists."

I got to the point that I would just as soon have suspended the veneer of egalitarianism and gone back to saluting and saying "sir." It would have done away with the guesswork.

The military training gave me a few advantages, however; some survival strategies transposed very well from one environment to another. My friend David Jordan, a fellow magazine editor who had been a communications officer on a navy destroyer, joined me in educating our colleagues in such proven techniques as:

1. Never walk anywhere in the building without a sheaf of papers in your hand, even if you're only going to the rest room.

2. Always stride purposefully wherever you go, even if it's only to the water cooler. And always seem to be rushing.

3. Always keep a half-written page in the typewriter (this was before computers), even if you're not working on anything.

4. Keep stuff on your desk. It's a myth that the neat desk evidences efficiency; it signals that you don't have enough to do.

It seems so silly in retrospect that we would have believed seriously in such trivial stuff, yet we did these things as if our bosses could be fooled or as if they actually gave a damn. But these were the years in which appearances seemed as important as results.

The Curse of "Us" Versus "Them"

These were also the years in which the only significant communication between employees and management was either formalized through labor-contract negotiation or contrived through understood social convention.

It was as if all management people had forgotten, or were conditioned to forget, that they once were "employees," that they once were at the bottom. Apparently, when they became "management," they changed from being "us" into being "them." There just was no institutionalized way of breaking down the barriers of old-time elitism and top-down authoritarianism.

Meanwhile, of course, there was a strong community within the institution, a rich culture of employees who not only worked together but who created a system of survival based on mutual affection and a shared suspicion of "management."

It was not unlike the fighter squadron with its pilots' suspicion and hostility toward the "wing weenies," who with all their charts and plans ended up doing what they always did: They sent us pilots out to do the real work, to fly, and sometimes to die.

And the good mid-level departmental managers in the corporation were direct operations managers, like those good squadron commanders and flight leaders who tried to harness the sense of community, to liberate the human spirit of the organization, and to turn it into the kind of shared endeavor that becomes productivity and bottom-line results, whether the bottom line is combat readiness or return on shareholder equity or some other measurement.

These were the years during which I saw and felt firsthand how old resentments—of the guy who owned the Weona grocery store and of the people in the mansions on Central who would not pay for their newspaper on time—play out in the workplace as resentment toward management. Despite my being a "manager" during some of those early years, I still felt the downward pressure and I still identified more with the workers than with the management.

Learning What Not to Do Is a Great Way of Learning What to Do

In those years, I learned all the rules of what management is not: Management is not a popularity contest; management is not about friendship; management is not about making people happy. But no one could tell me what management was, except of course the classic definition, "Getting results through people."

The biggest problem was that in my first management job, I became manager of most of my friends, so I found myself trying to go along with the conventional wisdom and practices of management, torn between being a boss and being a friend. My management style veered between authoritative and pleading, but settled after a while into a pretty simple formula that worked for a long time: Be sure people were clear about what we were going to do and what we were trying to accomplish, then identify the people who were having trouble and try to help them. I confess that I often invoked the old them/us dualism, setting management up as the oppressors and us workers as the victims. Though generally effective, what I did was more mechanical than spiritual.

This became a narrow and rocky path, and by the time I had been a manager for five years, I thought that I would never be able to move into a high-level management position. Why? I wouldn't have articulated it this way at the time, but I suspect it had to do with what I would now call the "class rage," or resentment of society's "haves," that I felt through many of my growing-up years.

The only two choices I had, as I saw them, were these: (1) Get out of management altogether, or (2) Do it differently. I chose the latter, and although up until that point I had learned only a little of what *to* do, the old command/control system—both military and civilian—damned well taught me every single day for years what *not* to do.

Confessions of an Accidental Businessman

Chapter Three

Bearing Witness

Our Mission is to liberate the human spirit at Herman Miller so that we can furnish to our customers environments in which to realize their full potential.

Mission Statement, Herman Miller, Inc.

We may not be, as some suggest, "called" to work. We may indeed start working to make money, to improve our status, to create a future, or just to stay off the dole, as they used to say.

I was very reluctant to get a job when I was a kid. I did not want to work. It seemed inconvenient, far too wasteful of my time. But we were poor. I did a little of everything— carried the morning newspaper on a regular route and then sold the afternoon paper on a corner to the businessmen who would stop in their cars on the way home from the office; chopped cotton and picked cotton on a farm; worked on a bread truck, on a construction crew, and as a soda jerk, waiter, copy boy, photographer's assistant, teletype operator, musician, reporter, and photographer—before I graduated from college. And this does not include my work scholarships as a university public relations writer, darkroom technician, and—yes, I got paid to do it—drum major of the university marching band.

Not one of those jobs did I do for anything but money. Not for training or education, not for the advancement of a career, not to create a productive future, and certainly not for personal or spiritual growth. Only for money (and occasionally for the chance to be around women, but that's another chapter).

My mother worked in degrading low-level jobs only because she had to make money. But I believe the reason that learning to operate the comptometer machine meant so much to her was because it evidenced a skill, the mastery of something almost mystical that elevated her to another plain of achievement, in her mind something like a professional. And of course, she credited God. She felt God had, as the old hymn said, planted her feet on higher ground.

Her belief that God had helped her did not stop there. God had helped her for a reason, and the reason was that she would now be in a better position to "witness for Jesus." This, in her view, was what we all were to do, those of us who called ourselves Christians.

"Jimmy," she would tell me, "you surely can use your paper route to witness for Jesus." Naturally I thought that to be impossible. What was I supposed to do, ask one of the people in the Central Avenue mansions or in one of the poor white shotgun houses, "Have you accepted Jesus as your personal savior?" or "Would you like to go to church with me?" I remember once or twice trying to summon the courage to approach the subject with one of my customers, but I did not have Mother's confidence that the Lord would save me from ridicule and embarrassment.

Confessions of an Accidental Businessman

The Importance of Doing Good Work

That is still my fear as I speak and write about the spirit of work, yet I know that the "liberation of the human spirit" in the context of the work we choose to do—even if we choose that work only for the money—is at the heart of the healing that must happen between management and employees if we are to save American business from a debilitating and destructive crisis of trust in the wake of all the reengineering and downsizing of the past several years.

No, it's not the same as witnessing for Jesus, yet I do believe that our work daily gives us our best opportunities to look for the best—the Divine—in others and to manifest the best—the Divine—in ourselves. Indeed, I believe any good work we do for or with others is also God's work.

Just what is good work with others? It is any work, no matter how routine or menial, done with generosity, positive intention, a spirit of community, and a commitment to doing it well.

What is good work done for others? It is anything done with unselfishness and generosity—a putting aside (or overcoming) of ego, for the benefit of another person.

But what if that other person is a jerk, a bad person, who doesn't give a damn for you or your good work? So much more the need for the courage I could not muster as paperboy and so much more the reason to try.

As Lao-tzu asks in the *Tao Te Ching*, "What is a good man but a bad man's teacher? What is a bad man but a good man's job?"

In previous books, I have described my skepticism of companies that make much public hoo-ha about their claims to conduct their business according to Christian principles, then use those principles to try to prescribe and control behavior and to repress their employees rather than to liberate and encourage them.

Yet I know of, and respect, business executives who do

use their religious principles to guide them in liberating the human spirit and in empowering their employees. I believe this is true of such American business leaders as Max DePree, author and former CEO of Herman Miller Inc.; his successor, Kermit Campbell; Peter and Jack Herschend of Silver Dollar City; Irv Hockaday of Hallmark; Mike Moody of AT&T; and Tom Chappell of Tom's of Maine, among others.

The Key for Managers Is to Remain Open to Human Connections

There is a certain uneasiness, a certain risk, in the subject of religion and business. Some of the risk is put to rest, I believe, by concentrating on the spirit in work, the opportunity it gives us to find personal and spiritual growth, rather than focusing on a particular sectarian interpretation of that spirituality.

But what does it mean, "spiritual growth?" I don't have a simple answer, and perhaps not even a good answer, but I believe spiritual growth has a lot to do with opportunities we have to connect on a deeper level with one another. I deeply want to believe that we find easy connection through our shared joys, but I know in my heart that the connections come most readily from shared loss and pain, and that is because in times of pain there is usually nothing to say to one another except the obvious which, I believe, leaves us searching for other expressions. Those expressions, if indeed we are open to the opportunities, may make appropriate the things we usually find difficult—a touch, even a hug, tears, a long walk, a note with a poem enclosed, the assurance that we will be thinking about our colleague or friend or employee, or praying for them.

A lot of trivia drops away when someone says, "I have cancer" or when someone's child is seriously ill or when a loved one dies. The only thing to do in those circumstances is show that you care. And that is not always easy to do.

I believe my own expressions of caring, though sincere, probably were very socially ritualistic until I experienced first-hand my own need for caring. By that, I don't mean that I had not needed caring attention and nuturing at various times during my life, but I don't believe I admitted the need for it, thus I had not consciously experienced the need for it.

That changed in the mid-seventies when my mother died, followed by the death of my stepfather ten days later. Until then, I used to question the value of sympathy notes and flowers, but when I walked into that little funeral home in Ripley, Mississippi, I was overwhelmed by the flowers from friends and co-workers.

The affection I felt expressed by the flowers and by the notes, as simple and obvious as those words were, was a revelation to me, and it awakened a recognition of connection that far transcended my previously held assessments of those relationships, professional and personal. In that recognition, I believe I experienced some inkling of the spiritual possibilities within the everyday relationships.

Since those times, I have approached every note of encouragement or of sympathy with as much thought and care, with as much attention to my words, and as meditatively and reflectively as possible.

Look for the Ineffable in Our Everyday Work

This is not to say that the possibilities for deeper connections come only at times of pain. There simply is no denying something ineffable just in the very act of working together and in accomplishing together what we set out to accomplish. I believe we feel this something but often don't recognize it, much less understand how to express it. We can't even put labels on it. We say we "love" our jobs, we find them "challenging and rewarding," we are "motivated," we are "team players," we take "pride" in what we do. Managers talk about "vision" and "excellence" and "quality" and "empowerment." We coach and are coached; we mentor and are mentored. We seek continuous improvement. We want always to be learning. We talk about ethics and integrity, about health and healing. We have all of this language, yet what does it literally say about that indefinable something we feel about what we have chosen to do? Very little. The same is true as we try to express those feeling through parties and celebrations and conferences, through pep rallies and retreats, through the simple act of an informal get-together after work.

But those who are willing to take a more metaphorical view will find that these superficial words and activities symbolize the most profound expressions of our deepest selves, and they will understand that we simply have not developed an adequate vocabulary for what we feel as we seek meaning and dignity and growth in the everydayness of our work and lives.

Among my regrets as a manager is that I did not develop a clear enough sense of this metaphorical view in earlier years and, when I did, that I did not do more to help my colleagues and employees find that meaning.

Certainly, I had no understanding about this as a young man, but I recognize now that several profound things were trying to make their way through in those years. One was a sense of worth and esteem I began to feel as a copy boy for the Associated Press. I would pronounce "The Associated Press" with an air of great importance, much the way Mother pronounced "comptometer." Later, I came to say "AP" as if every boy in my high school should know what those initials stood for.

The sheer size of the organization, its dominant place in the world of news gathering, the energy of the office— reporters shouting, photographers rushing still-wet photographs from the dark room, the noise of the machines and the absolute miracle of them—and my place as a cog in this great wheel gave me feelings I had never had. Never. I was no longer this kid who had few clothes, little money, no car, and no time to play sports because he had to work. I was "with" the Associated Press, and the Associated Press needed what I could do.

Be Open to the Experience of Community

Another dim understanding came in those moments when all of us—reporters, photographers, teletype operators, and I—had worked together and had beat the United Press with a story. We would stand at the teletype machine, watching it run as Harrell Allen or one of the expert teletype operators punched the tape, fed it into the transmitter, then with consummate skill punched the story fast enough to keep up with—and even gain on—the tape as it clicked through the feeder, sending it signals that appeared magically on the machine. It was a particular spirit of celebration if our story ran on the "A" wire, the national news wire of the AP. I could not have used the words then, or understood the concept they represent, but I was participating in the community of work and feeling the spirit of it.

The community was made all the more real at Christmas, when on Christmas Eve the various AP bureaus around the country sent their elaborate Christmas greetings over the generally idle machines. There wasn't much news to transmit, so the artists of the teletype were given the opportunity to exhibit their best work.

On my first Christmas, Harrell Allen asked, "Would you like to send your own Christmas greetings over the state wire?" I was overwhelmed. I was taking typing in high school in hopes of becoming a teletype operator but had never used the machines. Harrell set it up, and I carefully punched Xs into a simple pyramid design of a Christmas tree, and wrote, "Merry Christmas to all Tennessee AP staffers." I loved using words like "staffer."

"How shall I sign it, Harrell? Memphis Bureau?"

"Just use your own initials, 'JA/MX'"

I put the tape on the transmitter, then hit the toggle switch and watched the state wire come to life and print my message. I tore it from the machine, a two-inch strip of low-grade paper, took it home to show my mother, then kept it in a scrapbook for years. I realize now it was more than a memento.

I would not have said "more than a momento" in those days, however. For all the good feelings I was able to have in that clattering, carbon-smudged teletype room, it was to my mind still just a place where I went to work to make some money; and making money—not the human spirit, not the enrichment of the inner life, not grace—was still how I identified the meaning of my work life.

The Spirit Is at Work in All Kinds of Work

The air force seemed so different that I assumed there could be no connection between life as a fighter pilot and a civilian working in an office. The camaraderie, the identity, the special bonds of risk and death surely could not be replicated in some damned office building while wearing a suit and tie.

Of course, I questioned why some pilots got killed and I didn't, but the notion that it might have something to do with "grace" never entered my consciousness. A part of all pilots wants to believe that we could handle any situation and would not have been killed as others were. But that was not true. We talked a lot about luck, but I found myself doing a lot more praying in those years, traditional praying in which we bring our wish list for consideration. I think I would now classify that as being scared into religion, and I don't think it qualifies as enlightenment.

Back in civilian life, I became immersed in what it took me a long time to realize was not unlike the fighter squadron after all, but it was still "just a job." I've often wondered why it took so long to "get it," to realize what was really going on as my friends and colleagues and I turned to and busted our asses to do good work together, to get good results, to make our boss look good to his boss.

It was not until the early eighties when I was a senior corporate executive that I began to understand the power of the spirit in work, the need for community and connection among workers, the opportunity for growth of many kinds that work provides. I began to believe also that the manager's fundamental job—and certainly the thing that distinguishes managers who are destined to become leaders from those who are not—is to encourage that spirit and those connections. I came to believe that the long-term well-being of an enterprise and all its communities depends not so much on leaders who are great at telling people what to do but on leaders who will help people know how they are to be. In other terms, the leader's primary long-term focus should be *context* rather than function: how the people and the organization are to be, with one another, with their employees, with their managers, with their vendors, with their customers, and with their community.

I'm not sure how I came to these understandings. A lot was going on personally with me in the late seventies and early eighties. I was being divorced from my second wife, Dorothy, and I was feeling shame and embarrassment and a sense of failure because of it. During these years, I felt surrounded by illness. One of my best friends, Red Seney, and my older brother, Ronald, both came down with multiple myeloma; Red lived only eight months; Ronald lasted two and a half happy years. My elderly father was in declining health. And I was diagnosed with a blocked coronary artery.

Perhaps it was those traumas, being brought face to face with my own mortality as well as the mortality of people I loved, that led me to a more spiritual sensitivity. Perhaps it was the fabled midlife crisis. Undoubtedly all that had something to do with it. But I know it was also the strong influence of friends who began to lead me on more spiritual personal paths.

I began to understand the need to find meaning in the everyday things, to see the Divine in others, to discover holiness in the most mundane of activities. I wanted to know how to do these things, so I began with the help of others to study myth and eastern religions, subjects about which I was colossally ignorant. I went to seminars and lectures and retreats.

In 1982, four days before my brother died, I was married again. In the process of finally overcoming my embarrassment about divorce and the fear of marriage, I became even more in touch with my spiritual roots and reestablished a deeper relationship with the religion of my childhood than I'd ever had or thought I'd have—a relationship informed by a deep appreciation of other religious practice.

I began also to know in my gut that the inner life must not be separated from the work we have chosen to do, no matter what that work is. I knew that the only reasonable and healthy choice in work and life is to find the balance and, in turn, to help others find that balance. I realized that "burnout" is not a matter of working too hard, it is a matter of finding no meaning in what we do; not a problem of mental/physical energy but a problem of emotional energy; not a crisis of time but a crisis of spirit. As a friend puts it, "It is not that we bite off more than we can chew, it's that we bite off more than we can savor." More and more I knew that what most of us need is not a getting away from the drudgery of work but a getting into the joy of work, not a separation of life and work but an integration of life and work.

And to quote, as I have in previous books, Rabindranath Tagore:

> I slept and dreamt that life was Joy;
> and then I awoke and realized
> that life was Duty,
> And then I went to work—and, lo
> and behold I discovered that
> Duty can be Joy.

Confessions of an Accidental Businessman

These understandings or realizations or moments of truth prescribed for me a path that was quite different from the one most often used in business, particularly by senior corporate executives. Once again I found myself needing to come up with the courage to witness, and somehow it seemed more important than ever. Once I began, I found many fellow travelers and I found that virtually everything I had learned from my newsboy days through the air force days and into senior management pointed incontrovertibly in the same direction: toward the inside, toward the inner life, toward the ineffable.

There are many lessons about the spirit of work, and three of the most important are these: We should be thankful for work itself, we should be thankful for the people we work with, and we should recognize and be thankful for the grace of our spiritual possibilities at work.

✌ Recessions

Why do we keep on keeping on,
in the midst of such pressure,
when business is no good for no reason,
when everything done right turns out wrong,
when the Fed does something
and interest rates do something
and somebody's notion of consumer confidence does something
and the dogs won't eat the dog food?

What keeps us working late at night
and going back every morning,
living on coffee and waiting for things to bottom out,
crunching numbers as if some answer
lay buried in a computer
and not out among the people who
suddenly and for no reason
are leaving their money in their pockets
and the products on the shelves?

Why don't we just say screw it
instead of trying again,
instead of meandering into somebody's office
with half an idea,
hoping she'll have the other half,
hoping what sometimes happens will happen,
that thing, that click, that moment
when two or three of us
gathered together or hanging out
get hit by something we've never tried
but know we can make work the first time?

Could that be it,
that we do all the dull stuff
just for those times
when a revelation rises among us
like something borning,
a new life, another hope,
like something not visible catching the sun,
like a prayer answered?

Chapter Four

How I Learned That Customers Sometimes Think They Own Your Business

If going from college into the air force was more a transition toward adulthood than a choice of career, then the move from air force pilot to editor of *The Courier-Chronicle* in Humboldt, Tennessee, was my first step into the grown-up world of work. Not that flying jet fighters was not difficult and grown up work; it's just that, at my level, it was a job in which one's skill was the true determinant of one's success. There were no political battles, no turf, no organizational maneuvering.

The Courier-Chronicle was not exactly a hotbed of corporate politics either, but its relationship to the power elite of the town created situations that, even in my short tenure, demonstrated that my degree in journalism, with its smattering of courses in weekly newspaper management, was not going to take me far in the *business* of journalism. I discovered also that skill as a writer and editor did not necessarily translate into skill as a communicator.

Mr. Frank Warmath owned the newspaper as well as the radio station. I was in considerable awe of him when I interviewed for the job. He was the first rich person I ever worked for. My father-in-law at the time, a successful businessman himself, told me, "Warmath's daddy left him well fixed, but he's made a hundred dollars for every one his daddy left him. And his wife has more than he does."

Mr. Warmath lived in the finest house I'd ever been in, and it seemed to me that, just by working for him, I would have some status, some position, in the town, something I had never experienced. And I had the impression that Mr. Warmath wanted his editor to have that position. In addition, it was clear that he wanted to make *The Courier-Chronicle* a real newspaper and use it to help the town grow. Sounded good in every way to me.

I figured I would write a weekly column commenting on all the important considerations of the community, much as I did as editor of my student newspaper. We would have hard-hitting editorials about what needed to be done and who should do it. We would cover the news in our county as well as possible, given the limitations of publishing weekly instead of daily. And maybe someday we would become a daily or at least a semiweekly.

I showed up on a Monday morning and was introduced to the staff by Mr. Warmath. I discovered that I was the entire full-time editorial staff. Two people who worked in the front office did various clerical jobs and sold school and office supplies to the public. From time to time, they also wrote small articles. Bob Brownell, the business manager and chief advertising salesperson, also wrote articles from time to time, and he let me know right away that I was to sell advertising as well as work the front office during busy periods, usually right after school when the kids stopped by for poster board and other art supplies. And on closing and printing day, we all did everything, including hand-set headline type, make up ads, and handle materials in the print shop. All the makeup was by hand, and we printed on a monster flatbed press, which was fed by hand.

It was a busy place, and I quickly decided to postpone writing a weekly column. I never did become a columnist.

As for the editorials, there were some. Mr. Warmath was determined to persuade the airport committee to try for some federal funds to improve the airport. The runways were pot-holed and the small operations building, if it could be called that, was in terrible disrepair.

I mapped an approach. First I would take my trusty Rolleiflex camera and do a feature story on the sorry state of the airport. I did it and ran a big story in which I quoted businesspeople who asserted that they might be tempted to bring a new plant into Humboldt if only there were a decent airport. And so on.

Next in my plan was to write a hard-hitting editorial admonishing the airport committee to do something about the problem. (I actually thought in phrases like "hard-hitting.")

Then I'd skip a week, and if nothing happened, I'd interview the mayor and the chairman of the committee.

But something did happen. I got a call from Mr. Warmath. He was laughing. "The mayor wants me to muzzle you. I guess they got the message."

In fact, the airport committee went to Washington, got the promise of money, and returned with a plan to bring the airport up to date. As much as this whole story now makes me smile, it may have been the last time I ever saw such direct immediate results from any of my journalistic endeavors.

It did not take long to settle into the routines of the job. Early in the week, I sold advertising, carrying ideas for ads to various businesspeople in town, listening to their complaints about the paper, about Mr. Warmath, about one another. The grocery store ads were most difficult of all: They were complicated—a jillion little pictures of products with accompanying prices that invariably changed at the last minute every week as each grocer discovered the competition's prices—but this was the backbone of the advertising revenue, so every week we went through schedule contortions to accommodate the advertisers.

We were able to sell ads to the hardware store and furniture stores and, occasionally, to some farm-supply dealers and car dealers. We got some national advertising, which came directly from agents.

The business manager and I would try to dream up promotions in order to attract extra advertising, and there were promotional packages from various sources. I remember building a promotion around material from the U.S. Department of Agriculture, suggesting that the planting of multiflora rose could cut down on erosion and help save the soil, as well as provide cover for wildlife. I called on the local cotton gin/grain elevator folks in addition to the other farm suppliers. It was a fairly successful little promotion that week; little did any of us know what a scourge multiflora rose was going to become for many farmers.

Every day for lunch, Bob and I would go to Miss Bessie's cafe for a meal I can now only dream about. One day, I met a writer of some national prominence, Jessie Hill Ford, a resident of Humboldt. He was on a toot, as some liked to say, about having been given a ticket by the police chief for executing a U-turn on main street in his Volkswagen. I think Jessie believed that there was some instinctive distrust in town of people like him, who seemed not to really work for a living, and especially of people who, at that time, drove funny-looking little German cars.

"If I write letters to the editor, will you print them?" he asked me.

"Of course," I said, "if they are within the bounds of good taste."

"Even if they expose some of the hypocrisy of this town?" he asked.

"Of course, if what you write is reasonable and true."

"Okay," he said.

The next day, I received a long letter to the editor from

Confessions of an Accidental Businessman

Jessie. In it, he explained that he had gotten a ticket for what he'd seen many other people do. But rather than protest, he said, he would help the police chief in his quest to identify lawbreakers. Jessie then listed violations he had observed, with the license number of the violator. "Will you still print this?" he asked in an attached note.

I did print the letter.

The day after the paper came out, the police chief was at my door. And Mr. Warmath was on the phone. The chief wanted to know if I would print his letter to the editor. I said I would. He did not write one.

Mr. Warmath wanted to know what the hell I was doing, allowing a personal vendetta like this in the newspaper, printing unproven allegations, and so on. I told him I did not see how to refuse printing the letters and that the problem of selective law enforcement was pretty well known.

The next protests came from every single advertiser I called on for the next week's paper. Although the airport feature and editorial seemed acceptable, they thought the newspaper's role was to "build the town up, not tear it down"; plus I think they were no more taken with this writer and his Volkswagen than was the police chief.

Nonetheless, I printed Jessie's next letter and, as I recall, the next. Then I told Jessie I thought he'd made his point and that he should just send his letters directly to the chief from now on.

Meanwhile, some of our best advertisers were in an uproar, and I found myself trying to explain my editorial position and sell advertising at the same time. This was *not* a classic journalism school case study. It was Bob Brownell's good humor that helped save the day.

"It's certainly given us something to talk about over coffee," he'd say to the advertisers. Then I'd say, "And we're not going to publish any more of the letters."

There was not a great deal of pleasure during the frantic four months I worked in Humboldt. Nearly everyone—

advertisers, the police chief, the mayor, the ministers, and kids who wandered in to buy school supplies—wanted to tell me how to run the newspaper. I came to realize they felt it was their newspaper and that I was still an outsider.

I came to realize also that not everyone in town had the same opinion of Mr. Warmath, and some considered it just another act of arrogance for "Warmath to bring in some wet-behind-the-ears, smart-ass outsider" to run the paper. My preconceptions about being a journalist didn't help either. When asked to join one of the local service clubs made up of businessmen, I declined on the grounds that the newspaper editor should not be aligned with any particular group. I remember one man saying, "I suppose this means you won't join a church in town." There was no explaining the difference.

Although my journalism courses at the University of Mississippi put a lot of emphasis on weekly newspaper journalism, nothing prepared me for the human relations dimension of being editor of a paper that was in itself one of the town's institutions and one about which people felt passionately.

Still, I was doing fundamentally what I was educated to do. My plan was to keep my eyes open for the opportunity to buy my own newspaper in some small town in the South, meanwhile learning from the Humboldt experience and trying to build up some savings.

The problem was that, on seventy-five dollars a week (I had been moved up twenty-five dollars a week after the first couple of months), I was not likely to build up any savings.

And then another thing: I began to actively dislike the job. I recall a story about why William Faulkner gave up his job in the post office at the University of Mississippi. He is quoted as having said, "I just didn't want to be at the beck and call of every son of a bitch with two cents."

I began to not want to be at the beck and call of every advertiser with fifty dollars for an ad which then entitled him to his two cents' worth of opinion about what I should and should not publish. This, I decided, was not journalism. And

Confessions of an Accidental Businessman

it was not the newspaper business. Never mind that it was both; suffice it to say that I was not to gain that perspective for a long time.

So I began looking for a job. I called every friend I knew who had a job in any phase of journalism. One of those was Mary Lynn Booth, a fellow journalism student who was with the Meredith Publishing Company in Des Moines, Iowa. Her response to my call was to put me in touch with the national sales director of Better Homes and Gardens Books, Tom Textor. He was looking for a regional book salesman traveling out of Memphis. When Mary Lynn told me about the job, she said there would be some public relations aspects to it as well, at least a tenuous connection still with journalism.

It turned out that Tom was an ex-navy pilot; naturally, we spent most of our time talking about flying and not the job, although he did make clear that there was no PR, no journalism, just selling. He offered me the job; I turned it down.

"If I had not wanted to get into journalism so badly, I would have become a career air force officer," I told him.

He was very generous in his response and, after returning to Des Moines, told his friend Jim Riggs, the managing editor of *Better Homes and Gardens*, that if he had an opening for an editor he might consider this young southern guy.

It was one of those "right place at the right time" stories, and the next week I found myself wearing my best suit and minding my best manners, trying not to look like a southern hick—my worst fear at the time—among sophisticated people at a fancy restaurant eating steak and drinking wine. I didn't know what to say.

Unlike Tom Textor, these people, top editors at a national magazine, didn't give a whit about flying airplanes and weren't even impressed enough to wonder casually how it might have felt to fly a supersonic jet fighter. So I talked about the only other two things I knew, music and journalism.

Later I joined Jim Riggs and the editor-in-chief, Hugh Curtis, at Curtis' home on a snow-covered wooded hill. As we sat before a fire in a house that for its day was quite contemporary, and talked late into the night, I felt I was glimpsing another kind of life, one far removed from Lamar Terrace and from small-town Tennessee and, for that matter, from the so-called glamorous life of the fighter pilot. It was, I recognized, not a life built on money someone's daddy left him but a life built on accomplishment. I knew at once it was a life I wanted a part of.

I am not sure what I said or did, or what they saw, but they offered me the job—copy editor of *Better Homes and Gardens* at $5,600 a year. Plus they'd pay my moving expenses, including mileage for my car. There was medical insurance and a retirement plan and, after a period of time, a profit-sharing plan. Infinitely better than maybe being able to save enough money to make a down payment on a weekly newspaper somewhere and maybe being able to own it someday.

When I resigned, Mr. Warmath did not seem surprised. "I knew I wouldn't keep you long," he said. "You did a good job." It was the first compliment he'd paid me.

As for the folks in Humboldt, imagine how they reacted to "their" editor leaving to become copy editor, whatever that was, of one of the largest and most beloved magazines in the country! It may have been the only time I gave them any sense of pride.

Confessions of an Accidental Businessman

Chapter Five

Legends and Heroes

I made up stories as a child during World War II. My Uncle R. A. had been a telephone lineman for Southern Bell before the war, so the army assigned him to the signal corps. His mother and father were divorced years before mine were; that seemed to give us a special connection, and he had taken me under his guidance, more like a surrogate father than an uncle. Thus, he was my war hero.

I told the other kids how, on New Guinea, he and the other signal corps linemen had learned to climb palm trees by spiraling their way up the trunks so they would not be such easy targets for the enemy snipers. Never mind that the line they were stringing would have been wound around the tree as a result of such fancy climbing, a detail that never occurred to me. The important thing was that I wanted to make stringing line during combat as glamorous as flying a dive bomber or driving a PT boat. That was my story and I stuck to it through the end of the war.

I did not have to make up stories about my Dad the Baptist preacher but just tell the often-repeated story of how one night a member of his congregation called and asked him to go to a local beer joint and bring her alcoholic son home. Dad went to the beer joint where the young man, on seeing him and knowing why he had come, pulled a knife. Dad, as it was told and retold throughout the congregation, said to him, "I don't want to have to hurt you, Henry, so just give me the knife and I'll take you on home." Henry gave him the knife; Dad led the whole beer joint in a prayer, then took Henry home to his mother.

So what has this to do with my business life? Well, nothing beyond the obvious observation that both Dad and Uncle R. A. were just doing their jobs. And perhaps this: The world of work is filled with everyday legends and unsung heroes, and not just on professional sports teams or in the military. They are everywhere, in businesses, government agencies, not-for-profit organizations; they are in our neighborhoods, our churches, and our schools. We have but to learn to recognize them. Unfortunately, they may not be easy to recognize because they are not engaged in such stuff as stringing telephone wire on palm trees in a combat zone and confronting men with knives.

How to Recognize the Heroes Around You

At this point, I should offer a real definition of "legend" or "hero," but I'm not sure I can. Everything requires skill and knowledge, every job, every profession, every discipline. To be successful, every practitioner has to possess and demonstrate some minimum level of competence. But I believe that every area of endeavor also has its myths and beliefs, its codes of practice, its catechisms and rituals, its priests and prophets. In this swirl of people and activity, heroes and legendary people emerge. The *heroes* do what they do against the resistance of the system or the authority structure; the *legends* simply do what they do beyond any level of normal expectation.

I think of Katie Norris, who until her retirement held

several titled positions, all of which amounted to the same job: She kept the copy and layouts moving on schedule from the creative staff of *Better Homes and Gardens* to the production department. Not an easy job when it comes to rushing writers and graphic designers, who may be in love with every word and every layout and who resent being pressured by the forces of dirty commerce.

But Katie did it successfully for years and without offending any of those creative sensibilities. Her tools were humor, an unflappable good will, and a unique talent for lending a sympathetic ear about why such and such manuscript was late while still pressing for its delivery.

I believe it was George Bacon, the art director at the time, who christened her, "Katie the Mother of us all." To carry on this affectation (and affection), the design staff prepared elaborate Mother's Day cards for Katie and created hand-lettered placards for her wall.

I always wondered how Katie got the stamina, the energy, the consistent (and sometimes it seemed the incessant) good will. Later I learned that she had been a single mother and during World War II had been an instructor pilot in biplanes for a while, then had ferried combat-ready planes to the ports for transfer overseas. In retrospect, the copy and makeup editor job must have seemed easy as pie.

Sometimes There Are Legends at the Top

Speaking of pilots, my air force days were filled with stories of the legends: famous ones like Chuck Yeager, of course, or Bob Hoover or Scott Crossfield or Tony Lavier, but also less famous ones like one of my squadron commanders, William T. Whisner, who at the time was one of the few living aces of both World War II and Korea. The "Whiz Kid" he was called. But it was not his legendary air tactics and kills that made him a legend with us junior pilots, it was his skill as a pilot. He was just a superb "stick and rudder man," one of those pilots who were so smooth they made it seem as if the airplane was an extension of themselves.

He had been squadron commander only a week or so before the word was out. "Have you flown with Whiz yet?" the pilots would ask one another. Everyone wanted to fly with him as soon as possible. I remember flying his wing one night in bad weather, a situation in which a quick or uncoordinated move by the leader can mean serious consequences for the wingman. Colonel Whisner was so smooth I could hardly tell we were manuevering through all that black murk. Of course the word spread to the other squadrons as well. Everyone just knew he was the best.

Just as everyone at the Meredith Corporation knew that its CEO, Bob Burnett was the best: the best speaker, the best salesman, the best leader in corporate America. The public record was clear enough: The stock went from seven to 120, then split three for one, then climbed to 80 and split two for one. But that was only part of the story. Bob's ability to lift us up, through only the power of his words, was the real story. The stock performance came naturally on the heels of what we were able to accomplish as a result of being led to understand the power of our own potential.

Bob, a small-town Missouri boy, had started his career as an insurance salesman and car salesman. He came to Meredith Publishing Company, as it was called in those days, as a trainee in the advertising sales department. He never forgot those roots or the people who were his fellow trainees, despite the fact that he quickly moved ahead in the hierarchy.

He lived the values of honesty and integrity, and was as concerned about the welfare of the line workers as he was about the corporate officers, perhaps even more concerned.

Although it is a widespread management style these days to talk constantly to employees about earnings and stock prices, Bob knew that the average employee doesn't relate to a "vision"—if you can call it that—of profit, earnings, stock price, return on stockholders' equity, and so on. Of course he

Confessions of an Accidental Businessman

talked about profit, but this is what he said: "We don't have to talk about profit. Profit is like breathing. We have to do it to survive and to grow. But if we concentrate on the health of our company—on doing the right thing, on producing quality products, on serving our customers—profit, like breathing, will result."

I came to think of Bob as a spiritual leader, and if not that, then at least a preacher. Do I think this heroic voice would still be relevant to today's business? Absolutely. And thank God, Bob still serves on the boards of some of the country's largest companies.

Most Legends Are the Everyday Kind

Most of the time, though, the real legends are those lower in an organization, doing their jobs, not expecting to lead the company, and expecting no special recognition. In fact, it's not rare for an everyday legend to refuse recognition.

Harrell Allen, the teletype operator, was widely known as the fastest and most accurate puncher in the business. On a hot story, the reporters wanted Harrell on the machine, and sometimes they'd dictate the story directly, promising always to deliver a typed manuscript later because—as a good union man—Allen always pointed out, his fingers flying over the keyboard, "I'm not supposed to do this." But if we beat the United Press, he was not reluctant to walk down the hall and razz the UP guys about it.

Katie Norris, even now years retired, protests that she was just doing her job.

One summer, I worked on a construction crew, and one of my jobs was to carry buckets of mortar, called "buckets of mud," to the bricklayers. The chief bricklayer worked with such skill others would stop to watch, or bricklayers between jobs would stop by the site to watch him work, smiling and nodding their heads at the end of each run of bricks.

As his pile of mortar became smaller, he would yell

"Muuuuuud!" and I knew I had better be there within one minute. One day I asked him, "Ben, how do you do those bricks so fast and have them come out so good?"

"I just been doin' it a long time," he claimed, but of course that didn't explain it. And maybe he didn't know.

Just as I don't think a school bus driver whom the kids called "Toad" ever knew he was different or that he had become a legend of a school bus driver.

It had nothing to do with dramatic, life-saving heroics, but that didn't mean he wasn't heroic and life-saving.

When my now twelve-year-old son was only two and a half, we were told, after many tests, that he had autism. Thanks to an infant early intervention and preschool program in the Des Moines Public Schools, Ronald began to go to school before he was three years old.

Every morning, we would put him on a yellow school bus with a group of other children, all of whom had disabilities of one sort or another. Every afternoon, he would return on the bus. One day I was home from the office and met the bus. I had heard of Toad the bus driver but had never met him. As Ronald got off the bus, Toad said, "Goodbye, Ronald, I'll see you tomorrow."

Ronald was not yet verbal. He had a little sign language but could pronounce only the first sound of a word. For "Bye," he said something like, "Buh," which came out as little more than the "B" sound itself. That was all he could say.

I learned that day he and Toad had a ritual. When Ronald, who had motor skill problems as well, had laboriously climbed down the school bus step, he turned. Toad said again, "Bye, Ronald."

Ronald said, "Buh" and smiled.

Toad said, "Look at me, Ronald." Eye contact is difficult for many people with autism, and they must be encouraged and taught to make eye contact. "Look at me, Ronald," Toad said.

Ronald looked at him. Toad said, smiling and making full eye contact, "I love you, Ronald."

Confessions of an Accidental Businessman

Imagine that. This big school bus driver would, every single school day, engage my little boy's attention and say, "I love you, Ronald." I can't imagine that anything Ronald experienced at school in those days was any more important than his relationship with Toad. Try to imagine also what instinct, what knowledge, what wisdom moved Toad to make these connections with the children; for it is those instincts, that knowledge, that wisdom that I believe inspire the everyday legends and unsung heroes like Toad.

Certainly that was true of Ronald's first teacher, Twyla Wanek. My most vivid recollection of "Wanek" (as the kids called her) was of her down on her knees gently restraining a boy whose behavior had become overly aggressive—not an uncommon event in a class of children with autism.

She was firm in overpowering him in a way that would prevent his hurting himself or someone else, yet she was gentle and loving. At the time, most educators and concerned parents in Des Moines considered her the top "autism teacher" in the city.

"How did you learn about autism and how to teach kids who have it?" I asked her.

"The hard way," she answered. "When I first started working with these children no one even used the word 'autism.' No one talked about autism at all; maybe they didn't know what it was. I was just told that these kids were mentally retarded or had a behavior disorder or some combination. So I just started teaching them and worked it out for myself."

My most enduring impression of Twyla is that she was never still. She was on the floor or moving from child to child—speaking in her constantly upbeat, encouraging voice, always reinforcing the sometimes meager accomplishments of a struggling student, "Good job!" or "Look at me. Good looking!"—teaching every single second. I believe she knew and felt deeply that whole futures depended upon her willingness to do this work and her energy in accomplishing it.

And it took more physical and emotional stamina than most of us can imagine bringing to any job. I still wonder how she did it for so many years.

Sometimes It Takes a Trailblazer

One of my current business heroes is an executive at AT&T, Mike Moody, who at the time I met him was VP of sales for the West.

I first heard of Mike several years ago when Tom Hoffman, Mike's colleague, asked me to attend their group's conference in Bodega Bay, California. Before going there, I learned that Mike had put on a "personal growth fair" for these sales managers and was—get this—making "personal growth" a part of their performance standards. It was also his intention that an emphasis on personal growth make its way throughout the organization.

I was to speak in the late morning, and after sitting through the group's first two sessions, realized that I was seeing a *true transformation* among a business group of one of the best-known companies in the world.

Mike spoke, seemingly off the cuff, for forty-five minutes or so. He was clear in expressing his belief that an emphasis on personal growth would also produce good business results. Then, each manager rose to report on how personal growth initiatives were becoming part of everyone's performance standards. Some of the managers spoke of the "journey" they and their people were undertaking.

My first words after being introduced were, "You don't need me. You are the most evolved management group I've ever seen."

The other reassuring lesson was that Mike's group was leading the rest of the company's sales by double-digit percentages.

I know it required considerable courage and risk for Mike Moody to put aside the precepts of leadership under which he

Confessions of an Accidental Businessman

(and I) grew up in business and to blaze a brave new trail. There is no way I can know how much resistance he met, how many heads were shaking at corporate headquarters, how much pressure he felt to conform, of what promotions he might have not received. I know only that he is a hero indeed, and having had several sessions with AT&T people in his group, I know he has left an indelible legacy of leadership.

The Key Is in How They Engage Their Work

I have never been able to identify exactly what characteristics drive people to the kind of excellence that makes them into legends. But when they engage their work, something happens. I remember a photographer who, on the surface, seemed a great joker—as if he did not take anything seriously—but his photography was excellent. I worked with him one time and as we talked about the job, he seemed almost casual and inattentive. Then when we got to the location of the "shoot" and he began to set up, he turned serious. He and his assistant moved completely in sync.

"What happened to the jokes?" I asked.

He replied, "Well, when the flag goes up, the bullshit stops."

I think also of the late George deGennaro, a Los Angeles photographer of consummate skill and creativity who built his reputation as one of the top half-dozen food photographers in the world. I don't believe I have ever seen such focus except perhaps when Harrell Allen was punching the teletype. George conceived photographs, even the most commercial ones, to be works of art. And they were. As an editor, I used to lament about all the beauty that would be lost between George's glorious transparencies and the printed page. Ink on paper just could not capture them properly.

Getting to work with George deGennaro became a rite of passage for young food editors, and a successful shoot with him took on the importance of a graduate degree.

When George died, it was as if a light went out in our business, though I am happy to say he left a group of colleagues who had studied and learned as much as could be taught. That is, everything but the genius, the eyeball, the touch, the legend of it.

They Are Everywhere

When I open up to it, the everyday legends and unsung heroes whirl through my memory: the guy at Manale's Restaurant in New Orleans who opened oysters for 50 years. He made it look easy, and I used to order a dozen fresh ones just to watch him open them. Some people in New Orleans used to say you've never eaten a raw oyster until you've eaten one he has shucked. Or Stanley Baron, the advertising director when I was at *New Orleans Magazine*, who was legendary for never hearing the word "No." He could sell anything, and did. After almost being bodily ejected from an office, he would make his plans for the return call. His secret was simple: good humor and a good sense of humor. He did not take himself so seriously and he did not interpret a negative response as an indictment of him as a person.

Or David Jordan who, now coming to the end of his career in magazine publishing, may at last do the unique and superb woodworking and the microphotography of insects for which he has become an everyday legend. David almost made a career of taking on the toughest troubleshooting jobs in our company. I appointed him editor of *Apartment Life*, a struggling magazine at the time; then I sent him to Australia to help us establish a magazine down there; then I asked him to set up a video new-product operation; then he became editor of *Better Homes and Gardens* in a somewhat troubled time. Perhaps his greatest accomplishment, although one not likely to win him any great esteem from most businesspeople, was his work in establishing the Better Homes Foundation in support of homeless families. There is no estimating the amount of good this work has done for the health and education of homeless children.

I have always regarded David as the most competent person I know, and I think he came out of his lower working-class background in Peru, Indiana, believing that there was nothing he could not learn and do.

They Are Always Learning and Doing

Maybe it is that devotion to learning and doing that makes all the difference, that distinguishes the heroes, the everyday legends, from the rest of us. Maybe also it is the fact that they work to some inner expectation, to a standard that is far above the normal standard most of us expect of ourselves.

I spent a lot of years looking for heroes in all the wrong places. I kept expecting them to be always at the top, in positions of visible responsibility. I found them there, to be sure, but more often they were all around me. All I needed was the proper emotional lens, the correct spiritual context for seeing them. That lens, that context, turned out to be *gratitude*.

Once I learned to be grateful for heroes—like bus driver Toad who figured out how to love those noisy and unpredictable kids; and teacher "Wanck" who, at her retirement, had taught and touched the lives of hundreds of children with disabilities; and Katie Norris, whose real contributions were smoothing all the abrasive situations in a very abrasive business—I began to find them everywhere.

Of course, they were there all the time.

Still are.

✍ At the Air Aces Museum
—Falcon Field, Arizona, March 1995

After I find the photograph,
a pilot younger than I ever was
standing one foot in the cockpit, one on the wing,
smiling with six fingers in the air,
one for each enemy plane he had shot down
on that single mission when he dove into
a swarm of Messerschmidts,
I ask the office lady for his address,
eager to let her know the connection:
"He was my old squadron commander,
William T. Whisner, triple ace in Europe,
ace in Korea, one of six aces of both wars,
Bendix trophy winner, the Whiz Kid they called him,
I flew with him in the cold war."
She pulls out a book and runs her finger down a column.
"He died in 1989," she says
and tells me the circumstances,
about how the Whiz Kid, safely retired,
was caught by a surprise attack in peacetime.

In that last dogfight of my imagination
I can see him twisting, turning,
using all his old tricks to outrun them,
but he has lost his edge,
gotten rusty in the later years,
and one dives, turning inside him
and will not be shaken,
then as the Whiz Kid slows,
the killer gets just enough lead.
"An allergic reaction," the Aces Museum lady said.

Think of that,
of all the flying things that tried to do him harm,
Messerschmidts, MIGs, Fokkers,
and the Whiz Kid is shot down by a damned yellowjacket.

Chapter Six

The Journey into Real Management

It was a dreamlike experience, being escorted around the office by the Editor of *Better Homes and Gardens*, being introduced to the staff, some of whom were almost mythical names in the magazine business, being toasted as guest of honor at a welcoming coffee. How was I to know that my whole life was to revolve around my job and the company, that all those smiles and back pats and "welcomes" were accompanied by the expectation that I was to adopt a loyalty and dedication that, in retrospect, resembled servitude?

I started out nervous. I was nervous for at least the first three months. I recall joining a group of my new colleagues at lunch in the company cafeteria. Jim Riggs, the managing editor, joined us. Believe me, in the air force, the top officers don't eat with the junior officers. Riggs sat across from me, and though he probably was intent on eating his lunch and returning to the office, I felt he was watching me.

I had constructed a ham sandwich and, in southern fashion, had slathered it with enough mayonnaise to float the ham like a boat. When I bit into the sandwich—just as

Riggs looked up—a glob of mayonnaise plopped onto my plate.

Red Seney, who was to become one of my closest friends, quipped, "I thought you southerners were supposed to let the mayonnaise run down to your elbows rather than drop on the plate." Red was trying to save the situation with humor, but that was not the way I interpreted it. To me, it was a put-down, and I felt I had failed some cafeteria test and that I was thought of, after all, as an ignorant southerner. Afterwards, I decided to bring my lunch, to "brown-bag it" with my friend David Jordan.

As the weeks became months, it was with Seney and Jordan that I discovered I was not alone in my insecurities, in my sense of being overwhelmed by work, and in my need to make more money to support a growing family. When I discovered Iowa taxes and housing costs, the $5,600 a year in Des Moines began to look a lot like seventy-five dollars a week in Humboldt.

My sense of financial pressure made those early days at *Better Homes and Gardens* seem almost surreal. As copy editor, I attended all issue-planning meetings at which the creative departments proposed articles to be considered by the top editors for possible publication in the magazine. Thus I saw photographs of some of the most beautiful homes and furnishings and gardens and foods in America. These were things far beyond my life experience, and I couldn't imagine that very many people had enough money to afford to live in such surroundings.

What a strange and ironic twist that I, with my background, barely making ends meet, should be sitting among people who were regarded as arbiters of taste and style. I'll never forget an experience that stands still as an "Aha" moment for me.

It was in a home furnishings issue-planning meeting at which the top editor of that department was presenting what she said was a "budget decorating" story. "This article," she said with what struck me as utter disdain, "will be perfect for all the ladies in Beaverdale." At the time, I lived in Beaverdale.

So that was it, I thought. We're supposed to publish all this rich stuff most of the time, then every once in a while throw a cheap-tricks bone to the lower income folks. I can't imagine the color of my face, but I said nothing.

Later in the meeting, presenting a story on sofa beds, she referred to the "old jackknife sofa" as if the use of one should be considered uncivilized. What a supercilious bitch, I thought. I could recall that one of the most prized purchases my mother and I had made years before was a "jackknife sofa." It had meant I finally had a sleeping space to accommodate my growing teenage body.

Of course I was angry, and that meeting stuck with me a long time—long enough for me to resolve that, no matter how much success I might achieve, I would never forget where I came from, and if I ever were editor of a magazine, it would never lose touch with ordinary people.

I discovered that Meredith Publishing Company had a reputation for hiring promising young people and paying them salaries that, by magazine business standards, were far below the competition. Competitors in the magazine business who regularly hired away our good people benefited from the education those editors and advertising salespeople received from Meredith. The company's response was to hire more promising young people.

Seney, Jordan, and I—and there were many like us at Meredith—met this situation with humor. "Meredith is a great place to learn the business if your Mom and Dad can afford to send you here."

Meredith also had a reputation for never firing anyone, a practice that caused those who considered themselves highly competent to resent the incompetent people. We quipped about the "Meredith civil service."

Of course, had it not been for Meredith's practice of hiring relatively underqualified people then training them, I would never have been hired, and perhaps would have been fired. I was very uncertain of my qualifications to be copy editor of *Better Homes and Gardens*, but I could not confess my doubts even to Seney or Jordan. I had to be on a steep learning curve or sink. There was one saving grace: I worked like hell, night and day, to learn the job, and I did whatever Jim Riggs asked me to do. In turn, he was a pretty good teacher, both of what to do and what not to do.

Riggs was rather given to circumlocution, and his editorial decisions frequently required interpretation for the editors and writers. I learned that my predecessor had fulfilled that role and that it now would fall to me. With Riggs being from Missouri—almost southern—it was not difficult for me to understand his intent.

In just six months, events which I knew nothing about and did not anticipate found me once again in the right place at the right time. Riggs became executive editor of the magazine and decided that, rather than replace himself with another managing editor, he would split the job into copy and administrative functions. He promoted me to copy chief, a move that carried virtually no additional authority but was accompanied by a six hundred dollar a year raise. A raise after only six months on the job. Fancy that!

I was to be "boss of the copy," responsible for the writing quality in the magazine. Riggs hired another man, Jack Hess, who had been with a book publishing company, as administrative editor. Jack was to be "boss of the budgets."

Anyone who knows anything about a magazine's operation knows that creative work and budgets are not easily separated. Not many people on the staff expected this split responsibility to work. And it didn't. Hess and I, without being aware of it, had been thrown into a competitive situation in which the "winner" would probably become managing editor. This was the talk among the staff, but I just pooh-

Confessions of an Accidental Businessman

poohed it as all part of the rumor mill. Meanwhile, I continued to work like hell.

The editorial and design staff of *Better Homes and Gardens* often felt put upon by the business types in the company. We felt underpaid and overworked and, more important, undervalued for what we did. This feeling helped galvanize us into our own community, which had both healthy and unhealthy results.

We took a lot of pride in what we did, making a big national magazine, producing those stories and pictures that millions of people would read and, we hoped, be inspired by. We enjoyed the esteem of architects and interior designers and builders and homeowners (many of them rich) when we traveled. We were taken to dinner by photographers and given special attention by restaurateurs.

But when we were in Des Moines, we were, once again, employees of "Meredith's" (as the local people referred to the company) and felt value and esteem only among ourselves. The feeling of "us against them" was too much with us, and our response was to become too dependent on one another for our sense of well-being. We resorted to humor, which was good; we bitched, which was okay; and we drank, which caused trouble for some of us.

As a fighter pilot, I had learned a thing or two about "us against them," about living with pressure, and about drinking. I was to discover that drinking was also an occupational hazard in the magazine business, both on the editorial staff as well as the advertising sales staff.

The *Better Homes and Gardens* staff partied so hard and so often together that a group of us became known locally as the rat pack. This was in the early sixties, when Frank Sinatra, Dean Martin, Sammy Davis, Jr., and friends were widely known as the rat pack. We figured that we must be Des Moines' answer to that crowd.

At first we partied on the weekends, every weekend. Then a smaller group began to have Thursday night "get-a-jump-on-the-weekend" parties. We danced to Al Hirt and Herb Alpert and The Tijuana Brass, to "The Girl from Ipanema" and the music from "Never On Sunday." In the calmer moments, we had limerick contests and told stories and played skittles and touch football. In winter we went sledding—on one occasion sneaking onto the golf course of the most exclusive country club in town—nipping at brandy between every downhill run.

Some of it was good fun, but there was too much booze, too much close dancing with one another's spouses, and too much jockeying for position with our bosses. I saw that staff members who chose not to participate in the social life were not part of the "in group." The job became everything, and I began to feel that my success was tied as much to the parties as to my work.

It took years for me to understand the impact all those working hours and all that partying had on my marriage. Jackie and I spent very little time alone; we were either with our two young sons or were at some "official" function or were partying. The ironic thing, of course, is that we thought we were having fun, the enjoyable life of the typical American up-and-coming young career family of the 1960s. It's not difficult to look back now and see that we were headed inexorably for a crash.

But hell, at the time I loved it. I did not like working so hard, but I loved the idea of being a magazine editor, and I loved the parties. I was also developing some friendships that would last for years.

As for the jockeying, I had an advantage. I had learned in the air force about whisky talk. There was always some young pilot who would get drunk at the Officers' Club and tell the wing commander how to run the unit. It was not a good career move, and I was warned about it early on. So I never let the whisky make me try to tell Riggs or the creative director, Burt Dieter, how to run the magazine.

In about a year and a half, Jack Hess resigned from the

staff and after only two years with the company I became, at age 29, the youngest managing editor in the magazine's history: salary: $8,000 a year. All I had to do was take on Hess' former duties along with my own.

Learning the Difference Between Authority and Power

I have never kidded myself about that first big promotion. Riggs put me in the job because I was good at getting done what he wanted done.

But suddenly I had become one of "them." I was the manager of my closest friends along with the rest of the staff. It is at this point that I began the real management journey in which I tried to find my way through all the conflicting messages of management as well as through my own conflicting feelings about being a manager.

How was I to party and dance with these folks on Saturday night then crack the whip on Monday?

Any journalism student knows that the traditional nickname of a managing editor is "The Whip." I carried that mind-set with me into the job and felt that I was to assure that all the copy was well written and in on time, that the budgets were prepared and approved on time, and that the two—creative output and expenditures—were to balance.

I was quickly to discover the difference between authority and power. Technically, I had authority over some of those mythical editors who not only had built substantial careers at *Better Homes and Gardens* but also had influenced the entire field of magazine editing. These editors—Faye Huttenlocher, tablesettings; John Normile, building and architecture; Myrna Johnston, food; and Fleeta Brownell Woodruffe, gardening—were always gracious and courteous in editorial planning meetings and such, but they simply paid no attention to me. It was as if there was no managing editor. They went directly to Dieter and Riggs with ideas, photographs, and finished manuscripts. They went directly for budget approvals. I found myself processing their work much as I did as copy editor.

I got some glimpse of my status with them once at a party when Myrna, who apparently was something of a palm-reader, grabbed my hand, looked at it, and said with a laugh to Riggs, "Well he's smarter than I thought. Maybe he'll learn after all."

It was an embarrassing moment, and I was chagrined enough to demand of Riggs the following Monday, "Am I managing editor or not? Do those people report to me or not?" After perhaps an hour of Missouri circumlocution, I began to get the message that I had to earn the respect of those senior editors and that my authority would become frayed at the edges if I tried to push it too far with them.

I took the hint. I had to find a way to work with them so that the copy could keep flowing, on time and of high quality. I stumbled into a technique that served me for years: I simply asked them how they'd like me to work with them. I also asked how I could help them keep their departmental production going smoothly. The results were amazing— another defining moment in my development as a manager— and at the time of their retirements, I had become close with all those highly visible editors.

But early on, as I struggled with not having authority over them, I was left with authority over the less-visible staff members, most of whom were friends or close acquaintances and most of whom were as deep into the financial struggle as I was.

I was not even sure what it meant to have authority "over." For that matter what did being the boss mean? My bosses had always told me what to do, when I was to come to work, when to go home, when to take breaks. When I was paid by the hour, they had authorized overtime. And more than anything else, they always seemed to be watching to see how I was doing what I was supposed to do.

In the air force, a pilot's mission would seem to be fairly clear-cut, yet we spent a lot of effort "filling in the boxes," making sure we had so many of this kind of mission and that kind of mission, so that when our inspections came, the inspecting officers could review those records and assure headquarters that we had fulfilled the requirements.

There was a distinct pattern of bosshood in the air force. It always seemed that the squadron commander was upbeat, a pep-talker. He mingled with the troops and talked to us about being the best. He never seemed to talk about filling in the boxes. That was left to the administrative officers. They were the ass-kickers, the box-watchers, the men to deal with. It had reminded me of a daily newspaper where I worked for a while. The editor was an Olympian figure who, we thought, was always contemplating the lofty goals of journalism, and the managing editor was the ass-kicker, the deadline-watcher, the man to deal with, the whip.

These were the only models I had when I became managing editor. There were no job descriptions, no standards of performance, no goals and objectives, none of the stuff we are so used to in corporations today. But my understanding was clear: I was to do, in effect, whatever Jim Riggs wanted me to do. It was clear I had no authority over the senior editors, and I did not want to be a whip, an ass-kicker, with all the people who had supported and taught me in my first two years.

As in any management position, a part of the job is representing senior management to the people and representing the people to senior management. It turned out that this became my major responsibility.

Dealing with the Pressure to "Do Something"

In the sixties, magazines were in a great depression. Television had captured the imaginations of consumers and the dollars of advertisers. And television was almost miraculous in its ability to get people to buy products. Arthur Godfrey could hold up some product and just sneer at it, and the next day stores all over the country would be sold out. Magazines were dying on all sides, even magazines that had been considered American institutions in their day: *Life, Look, The Saturday Evening Post, Colliers, Woman's Home Companion, Liberty*, and many others. Some media people questioned whether magazines could survive, so at *Better Homes and Gardens*, something of an American institution in its own right, the pressure was on to *do something*.

The risk of this kind of pressure is always the same: that you'll do the wrong thing but you won't find out until it's too late. We found ourselves divided into two schools of thought. One view was that our reputation had been built with our reader customers by our providing a certain kind of editorial material, so we should just keep doing what we had been doing, only better, and hope for better days.

The other view was that the world was changing, that our reader customers were becoming more sophisticated and did not want the same kind of magazine, even one done better. Riggs and Dieter, the creative heads, were divided.

I did not know which we should do. Riggs wanted to make big changes, so I supported him. I found myself in the midst of a sometimes uncomfortable competition between two strong creative visions. My counterpart on the design side was the magazine's art director, George Bacon, a brilliant artist, an irreverent, impish colleague, and a gentle and decent person. It often fell to George and me to interpret for the staff the directions coming out of the numerous planning meetings at which the editors would present their ideas to Dieter and Riggs. Sometimes, up against deadlines, we had no choice but to make our own decisions and risk that we would offend either Dieter or Riggs, and perhaps both.

George and I escaped into humor. In planning meetings, one of us would compose the first two lines of a limerick then pass it to the other who was then challenged to finish the lim-

Confessions of an Accidental Businessman

erick before the meeting ended. All this was made to appear as if we were dutifully taking notes.

George did junk sculpture and turned his office into a virtual gallery. He played guitar so we sang folk songs (these were the days of hootenannies) during the lunch hour a couple of days a week.

Despite my managing editor title, I felt I was still one of the troops, one of "us" not one of "them." When, as a result of my new duties, I learned the salaries of other editors, I even became a little resentful, feeling that I was the best bargain high-level editor they could ever have and feeling also that "they" really did not value the managing editor position. Hell, I figured I wasn't being paid enough to be anyone's boss. This, of course, was just an easy way out, a convenient rationalization for not engaging the authority and power issues.

These were years prior to Bob Burnett's tenure as CEO, and the system, if you could call it that, seemed driven by personality from top to bottom, from CEO on down. People went in and out of favor for reasons I could not discern. I found myself supporting and participating in all kinds of actions involving people's careers and incomes, actions based on nothing more than personal impression or a perceived personal loyalty or disloyalty. Or on judgments of character or personality.

One of my reponsibilities was to approve the secretarial salaries as recommended by the secretary supervisor. The pattern was clear: she gave the larger increases to the secretaries she liked and smaller increases to the others. Once I noticed that she was skipping one secretary in the raise cycle.

"Why?" I asked.

"Well, I don't know how to say this," she said.

"Just say it."

"Well," she started, then flushed and looked at her hands, "she's just a little bitch."

After letting that sink in a minute or so, I asked, "What does that mean? That is, what does she do to give you that impression?"

"I think she just dresses too sexy and is always flirting with some of the men around here."

I overruled her on that one saying that, if she feels the dress is inappropriate she should talk to the secretary or write her a note, but we would not skip her raise. Later, the supervisor complained to Riggs who told me, as gently as possible, that I should trust the supervisor's judgment in these matters.

I came to feel that salary increases, or the lack of them, were arbitrary as hell. Also—as a kind of subterfuge, I now realize—they were usually awarded in dollar amounts rather than as a percentage of income. When informing people of their salary increases, I would often tell them how much it worked out to per month, after taxes. That was the way I evaluated my income and my salary inceases, so I concluded this to be the most meaningful for everyone else. At that time, what did I know about percentages?

Decisions were so personal, often made after a direct private appeal by some staff member or the other, that George Bacon and I frequently felt we were the sweep-up crew, trying to straighten out the fallout from the most recent private decisions.

Humor Beats a Bitchy Memo Every Time

And there came those times when I couldn't just ignore problems of writing quality or with deadlines or budgets. I had to do something. By the conventional wisdom, I should have met with the person and written a memo expressing dissatisfaction with the work, or perhaps resorted to probation or some other disciplinary action.

I didn't want to do it, and though I knew what the management books said, I didn't really know how to do it. Also, it seemed to me people were working hard and it would have just felt unfair to come down on them for falling short somehow.

Still, often in frustration, I did my share of bitchy memos, always signing them "cordially" of course, and sometimes hiding behind a memo instead of meeting directly with the person. I admit that it was difficult for me to make my point stick in person. I was an easy touch; eveyone's stories always sounded so reasonable that I could not make life hard for them. So when the transgressions built up enough, I wrote a memo. The problem was that the memo's greatest effect was to make the recipient angry.

There was on the staff at that time a woman named Elizabeth D. Craster, who recently had come from New York where she had worked on several New York magazines. Personal circumstances had caused her to accept a job in Des Moines, and I think her perceived decline in status was an embarrassment. She was eccentric and effusive and extravagant in dress and manner, yet she was enormously talented as a writer and was sharp-tongued and witty.

At first, Liz irritated me with all her New York talk and her allusions that her exile in Des Moines would end as soon as she could get an appropriate job with a "real" magazine. It took a while, and the insight of a friend, for me to understand the desperate nature of this talk and how important it was for her to feel that she could always go back whenever she decided to. Before I reached that understanding, however, she became a target of opportunity for my management frustrations. No one particularly liked her, she did not "feel" like part of our group, and her eastern arrogance became reason enough to exclude her from my goodwill.

One of her responsibilities was to purchase props for photography, particularly china, silver, glassware, housewares, linens, Christmas decorations, various crafts objects, and so on. She was always over budget, sometimes spending the entire year's budget in the first six months.

Liz did not have the status of a senior editor, so my authority comfortably extended to her. God, I sent her some awful memos. My best stinging rhetoric. Words like *inconsiderate* and *irresponsible* and *profligate*. I threatened probation and worse.

Her reaction was to hide from me. If there was no escape and she had to walk past me, she would turn her head and look at the floor. Once I saw she was actually shaking, and I did not feel good that in her mind I had become such a bully. Still, I felt she brought in on herself.

David Jordan, as he did many times over the years, led me toward a better understanding of her by explaining her family situation, the loss of a great deal of money, a divorce, trying to live and support her daughter, and so on.

"But damn, David," I said, "she is driving me crazy with her budget problems and is causing a lot of trouble in the prop room."

"Talk to her," he said.

"I don't want to hear all her when-I-worked-in-New-York bullshit," I said, "and if she calls me 'dear boy' again I might yell."

"Well try something else, then, because I've talked with her and I think she is seriously on the verge of a breakdown. And you have become the catalyst for it, like it or not."

David's report of her story stirred in me the old memories of my mother's struggle after the divorce and the feelings I had when her bosses threatened her and she faced the loss of a job.

So once again, I turned to humor. I wrote her this memo:

> Dear Liz:
> I have this fantasy. It is about a china and glassware salesman who is outlining for his boss an upcoming sales trip.
> "I plan to hit Cleveland and Cincinnati first."
> "Good plan," says the boss.
> "Then I plan a whole Midwest tour, all the usual stops: Chicago, Minneapolis, St. Louis, Kansas City, LIZ CRASTER, Omaha, Topeka, and Denver."
> "Great plan," says the boss.
> I really think that some of those sales guys think of

Confessions of an Accidental Businessman

you as a major stop on the tour. I hate to cut into
their sales bonus, but do you think you could become
just a minor stop on the tour and not try to be right
up there with Chicago and Minneapolis and the
others?

I'd be happy to help if you'd like me to.

Cordially,

There were no threats, just the funny little story and an
offer of help. We got together, had a glass of wine over lunch,
laughed about the memo, and worked out a way that I could
help her with expenditures. Before her death some fifteen years
later, we became friends and, from time to time, confidants.

This experience was almost an epiphany for me, one in
a series of experiences that let me blunder and ricochet into
a way of managing that served me well for many years: I simply began to help people, to work with them on copy or figure the budgets for them or squeeze more time into the schedule. And by and by, the job of managing editor began to feel
more comfortable, though I became resentful of being the
clean-up crew and began to feel I would be doing that forever.

So I became restless. The notion of grassroots journalism was still in my blood at that time, 1966. The country
seemed in motion; there were big changes in my home country, the South. A part of me wanted to be there.

I had corresponded for a few years with Jim Townsend,
the founder of *Atlanta Magazine* and the person generally
regarded as the "father of city magazines." In 1966, he was
about to found another city magazine, this one in New
Orleans. He called and asked if I would consider leaving the
comfort of a major national magazine job to become editor
and publisher in New Orleans.

By early 1967, I was on the job in New Orleans with
the expectation of part ownership in the magazine, a shot at
real grassroots journalism, and the chance to be *the* editorial

decision maker. In a few months, I talked George Bacon into joining me as art director. It was to be a kick. Instead, it turned out to be a kick in the ass; the first big, and perhaps the best, step toward becoming a businessman. It required one initial understanding which, for some reason, over the years had not penetrated my professional journalist mentality: Journalism is, by definition, commerce. It is not art, it is not public service, it is commerce. That was a hard lesson to learn.

Chapter Seven

Learning to Be a Real Man in Business

Given my mother's struggles, you might think I would grow into the kind of man who was sensitive to the plight of women in the work world. After all, I had seen my mother fall into tears many a day after returning from her office at the Memphis Light Gas and Water Company to our little three-room apartment at 602-J Camilla in Lamar Terrace. It often turned out the men in the office had "kidded" her. It was a long time before I understood what that meant.

It was all Mother could do to pay the rent, buy clothes and school supplies for me, dress herself appropriately, buy groceries, give her tithe to the church (struggling always with the definition of "tithe"), and come up with eleven cents every Saturday so I could see the double feature matinee at the Linden Circle theatre.

Her greatest goal seemed to be that I grow up to be a "Christian gentleman" and that she be able to hold her head up and look people in the eye and not be ashamed of her life. This meant, I think, that she wanted to move some day from the federal housing project—"just a slum" she called it—to a house in a nice neighborhood.

Although I don't know for sure, I believe she also thought she might find a good man to marry. She dated a bit, sometimes bringing home a man for me to meet, then strolling with him to the benches on the playground, where occasionally I sneaked into the bushes to watch them kiss.

But there seemed not to be many good men around. In fact, as I think back on it now, I realize that, in those years during World War II, she went out with a series of the sorriest sons-of-bitches you can imagine. I used to play the pest so they would bribe me with movie fare to leave them alone. How was I to know they just wanted to get my mother into bed. Did they succeed? I don't know.

I do know about the tears and the depression and the courage and the pride. I do know about bosses who hassled her and married men who told her they were getting a divorce. I know about strangers who propositioned her even as she was walking hand in hand with me along the street. I know about her getting fired because she did not vote the way her supervisor wanted her to vote.

She did marry again, eventually, to a widower with two children. We all moved into his house in a modest neighborhood. As it turned out, he was mean as hell, took Mother's paycheck as his own, and slapped her around a bit when he was irritated. His children did not seem offended; apparently he'd done the same to their mother.

I was scared of him. He was a large, red-haired man who always seemed angry and menacing. When he was unhappy with me, he locked me out of the house for the night. I slept in the park.

Mother filed for divorce after only a year, and at the age of fourteen, I got to testify in court for the first time. I was so nervous I could hardly hear the questions. I was told later that the high point of the trial came when the opposing lawyer

Confessions of an Accidental Businessman

asked me, "Why, Jimmy, when this man opened his home to you, did you rarely speak to him?"

"Because he never spoke to me."

The divorce was granted, and once again Mother, a two-time loser in marriage, was challenged to hold up her head among her lady friends in church and at Eastern Star at a time when divorce was not common.

You can imagine how she then was treated by men in a series of subsequent jobs. Divorced twice! Can you imagine what the men thought and said? "Wow, she must be hot. One man can't keep her satisfied." And so on.

How, you may wonder, could I possibly know what those men were thinking and saying fifty years ago? Simple. Because my co-workers and I thought and said similar things about women, and that was only twenty-five years ago.

The Feminists Were Right About Testosterone Poisoning

By the early 1990s, in a senior management position, I had fired several men for sexual harassment; but if the same laws and rules and understandings had been in place back in the 1960s and into the early 70s, I could have been hanged by my thumbs for my attitudes toward, and treatment of, women.

I can't explain how I could have come to such attitudes. Just regular American male macho stuff, I guess. I agree with the feminists who call it testosterone poisoning. Clearly, it was thoughtless and without rationale and, ninety percent of the time, even without direct sexual intent. I certainly cannot remember ever discussing with another man the attitudes we should have toward women with whom we worked or how we should treat them, and companies made no mention of this in personnel policies or in new employee orientation manuals, except to the extent it was covered by certain prohibited behaviors.

Hell, my men friends and I were living clichés of young American professional males. We acted as if we were playing some competitive game, just as most of us had behaved in college and in the military. Women were allowed into the game only to do things that men would not want to do.

On the staff of *Better Homes and Gardens*, for instance, all the key positions were held by men. Women ran the food, home furnishings, gardening, and tablesettings departments, and men ran the building and remodeling and the features (travel, health, finances, and so on) departments. The art director and all but one member of the design department were men.

The clerical, administrative, and other such functions were done by women. I suspect most companies in the sixties reflected this kind of gender mix in position and function.

I remember when Betty Friedan's *The Feminine Mystique* appeared. Most of us men were more confused than anything else by its message. This is an old story by now, almost quaint in fact, but most of us lived in a world of assumptions that were constantly being reinforced by every institution, from business to the church to marriage itself.

For instance, I assumed that my position in the work world was permanent, whereas most women—except "old maids" and lesbians—were there only until they could find a husband and thus had no real lifelong obligation to work.

I assumed that I should be paid more than women in comparable positions because I had a family and they did not. As managing editor of *Better Homes and Gardens*, I regularly supported paying newly hired women less than newly hired men, regardless of qualifications and educational background, the rationale being one only of family situation. Oh, I remember one case in which we made something of an exception for a married woman because, apparently, she was supporting her child and "professional student" husband.

I assumed that secretaries were there to serve me. They were to make the coffee, keep my desk and office stocked

Confessions of an Accidental Businessman

with supplies, and run all kinds of errands from buying snacks to picking up cleaning to shopping for personal gifts. I always put it this way, "Would you mind . . . " doing such and such? And I would always thank them. But could they even consider refusing or suggesting that they had their own personal needs to fill or that what I was asking was inappropriate? Of course not.

(I do not mean to reject, or disapprove of, those situations in which secretaries or administrative assistants can so respect what the boss is doing that they want to perform such menial tasks in the interest of saving the boss some time and hassle. But I also think it is sometimes incumbent upon the boss to do little things to save time and hassle for the secretary or assistant—also as a sign of respect.)

My young professional men friends and I constantly used pet names with our secretaries and female co-workers: Dear or Sweet or Love or Hon or even Kid or Kiddo. What makes all this even worse in my recollection is that it was so thoughtless, so second nature. It was not that we wondered how women might react to all these names; to the contrary, we didn't give it a thought.

What a shock it was in the early seventies when one of the women in my department told me matter-of-factly one day, "I don't like to be called sweetheart."

"What do you want to be called then?" I asked, with a bit of edge in my voice."

"My name will do just fine," she said.

Generally, women who did not respond "appropriately" were thought to be having their menstrual period, and if they regularly refused to be coopted into playing a role somewhere between pet and personal servant, we tough young men might call them "ball-busters"and "bitches," though it would be unfair and inaccurate to say that was always our reaction.

In other words, all that stuff people in the early women's movement were railing about was very well justified. I am embarrassed and ashamed even now, as I write this, to remember how condescending and patronizing and what a generally insensitive jerk I was.

Sometimes Insight Hits You Between the Eyes

So what happened? Four things: two events, a process, and an event.

In the early seventies I was divorced and, shortly afterwards, married again. I have wondered many times how my first wife, Jackie, and I went from that innocent clinging to one another in a French whorehouse hotel on the first night of my military duty in France to a Des Moines, Iowa, divorce court fourteen years later.

I think my career had a lot to do with it. After three very happy years with the air force in France and that short time as editor of *The Courier-Chronicle* in Humboldt, Tennessee, I started my magazine career. As I pointed out in the previous chapter, I felt over my head as a beginning magazine editor; but, years before, when I found myself very much dependent on my own resources, I had developed the attitude that I could do anything anyone else could do if I just had a way to learn how.

It was not easy, and I had a lot of anxiety that I would not be able to keep up and would lose my job. My work schedule during most of the sixties was to go to the office at eight AM, get home about six PM, have dinner, spend some time with Jackie and our two young sons, watch the ten o'clock news, then get out my briefcase and work until one or two AM. I did this from Sunday through Thursday nights every week for several years. I often went to the office at some point on the weekend as well.

Money was scarce for us. My salary at Meredith was not enough, so I also joined the Iowa Air National Guard, taught adult education classes in writing, did substitute teaching at a colleague's night classes in freshman English at Drake University, and did some freelance writing and photography.

In other words, I was a lot of things in those years but I was not a father or husband who spent much time with his family. What little free time we had as a family was spent on good things: picnicking, fishing, cookouts with friends. And we took those long, driving vacations so popular in those days.

But our adult recreation was not so healthy—partying, dancing, staying up all night, chasing after some perception of lost freedom, then feeling remorseful as well as physically drained the next day. And those unhealthy days made for unhealthy conversations ranging often into accusative arguments.

Oh, it was easy to take the victim role; to be sure, I waxed righteously indignant with Jackie about all that I was expected to do. And of course I blamed it on my job with its demands and on my wife with her demands. But who knows the real reasons, how these things begin, what complicates them and then drives them toward the point of no return?

Obviously, my job was not the villain. Nor was my wife. Nor was I. There was no villain just as I was not really a victim. The circumstances were highly pressured, and my reaction to those circumstances probably was the single greatest cause of stress in the marriage. This was not the only cause or maybe even the most important cause, but with the clarity of retrospection, it is easily the most identifiable cause. I will not speak for Jackie, but certainly I found every excuse not to take responsibility for my role in our problems, and I was not smart enough, or informed enough, to try the psychotherapeutic alternatives available.

If my first marriage failed because of what my career did to me and to our marriage, then it may be true that my second marriage failed because it was more about careers than about marriage. I married a fellow writer and editor, a beautiful, well-educated, hip, smart, and savvy New Yorker who was to teach me a lot about all the stuff New Yorkers care about: the media world, art, design, what's hot, what's not, political causes, fashion, restaurants, food, wine, joyful and extravagant entertaining, and spending money. It was a hell of a long way from Lamar Terrace in Memphis.

Dorothy was a field editor for one of the Meredith magazines, and we met while working on a photo shoot together. I was entranced, and we were married. I have always said we probably would not have married had I not been the editor of *Better Homes and Gardens*, living in Des Moines, Iowa, at the time. It was, after all, the unconventional seventies, the great era of "living together" and other alternative arrangements.

But we married, and she moved from East 56th Street in Manhattan to rural Iowa, an area known as "west of West Des Moines." Our first big disagreement concerned women's rights, and I credit her with really getting my attention on that subject and educating me about the core issues.

The process of my development was also related to the times. There surely was something about the whole social environment of the sixties and early seventies that had a gnawing, building effect on me. As a white southerner trying hard not to be considered a white southerner in those days, I remember people in the women's movement equating their positions with those of black people. At first, I was offended by the comparison. I had seen, and been a part of, the discrimination against African Americans in the South. I had seen their exclusion from schools and churches and from participation in their government. I had seen the inequality of pay and professional opportunity between blacks and whites doing the same kinds of jobs. At first, the comparisons the women were making did not seem valid. It seemed to me arrogant and insensitive of women to borrow the victimhood of blacks and ascribe it to themselves. (At the time, I had no knowledge of the suffering and physical abuse visited upon the women in the suffrage movement of the early part of this century.)

Then, as my career progressed and I came into professional contact with more women, I guess I just began to pay attention. I read books and articles, of course, and I listened to speeches. But I believe the most important and persuasive impact came from watching and listening to the reaction of men as the women's movement gained momentum. It reminded me of some southern white people in the early sixties and their complaints about the restlessness of blacks. It was so common then to hear, "They don't want to be equal, they want to be more than equal."

In the seventies, I heard these same words said about women (as today I hear them said about gays and lesbians). Men were greatly offended by the presumption that women could perform in any job as well as a man and by women's increasing insistence on being paid the same wages. As the momentum built, so did the resistance until I could detect an almost seething resentment of women. Speaking as a man and not as a psychologist, I observed that the men who were most resistant seemed to be those who feared any kind of change and those who did not seem particularly comfortable in their masculinity.

As the nastiness increased, so did my impression that this was exactly like the racial talk I had heard so few years before. I remember talking with my close professional friends like David Jordan and Red Seney about how strange it was to see so many men become bent out of shape about women's rights.

And if men were threatened and angry, what of the older successful professional women who had succeeded in business by the old rules and who felt that younger women should be able to do it in the same way? And the women who had at some point given up a career to stay home and fulfill their "duty" as women and mothers?

In many ways, it was a very strange time, and I confess I was having trouble bringing my own attitudes and behavior into congruence with what I increasingly understood to be a new paradigm in the social makeup of the workplace. It was not that I resisted it—I did not—or that I did not feel it was right—I did. It was more a matter of not feeling that I really had a lot to do with it, despite my steady advance up the corporate ladder during those years. I guess I just wasn't ready to face it yet, at least to the extent of asking myself what I should do about it.

And then, the defining moment: My mother died.

Before the funeral, I went to the cemetery to see exactly where the grave was being dug. I expected to find some kind of large yellow machine scooping up the North Mississippi red clay; instead there was a big African American man digging with a spade. I introduced myself. His name was Otis Cox.

"Mr. Cox," I said, "I thought they used machines to dig graves these days."

"Yes they do most of the time," he replied, pausing with his foot on the shovel and wiping his sweat with a handkerchief, "but Miss Ruth was always very nice to me, and it don't seem right to dig a grave with a machine if you knew the dead person."

Mr. Cox wanted there to be nothing impersonal about his last connection with my mother, and in my grief it struck me that very few of my mother's contacts with working men had been this loving.

This was another of those epiphanies that, combined, add up to the wisdom we acquire in life. It shocked me to realize that I had somehow let myself forget or discount my mother's work experiences as if they had no relevance to my life and my work and the people with whom I worked, particularly the women. I felt as if I had let myself become just a part of another generation of men like those who harassed my mother. I had some extra bad moments in that cemetery and at the funeral and during the weeks that followed. There was no way, of course, that I could take back my behavior, that I could make it up to my mother or any other woman. I probably could not change old attitudes very quickly. And I probably would continue to struggle with the old sexual feelings. But I could change my behavior personally and I could effect change in the work environment.

Confessions of an Accidental Businessman

✐ Grave Digger

His name is Otis Cox
and the graves he digs with a spade are acts of love.
The red clay holds like concrete
still he makes it give up a place
for rich caskets and poor
working with sweat and sand
in the springing tightness of his hair.
Saying that machine digging
don't seem right if you know
the dead person
his pauses are slow as the digging
a foot always on the shovel.
Shaking a sad and wet face
drying his sorrow with a dust orange white handkerchief
he delivers a eulogy

Miz Ruth always gimme a dipper of water

Then among quail calls and blackeyed Susans
Otis Cox shapes with grunt and sweat and shovel
a perfect work
a mystical place
a last connection with the living hand

Not Everyone Wanted the Changes

It was shortly after Mother's death that I was asked to address a professional society of home economists, many of whom were my employees. I decided to talk about women's liberation. Even though the audience was entirely working women, they were nonetheless surprised, if not shocked, by the choice of subject.

I remember closing the talk this way: "Think of a dual control airplane," I said, "in which the controls must be manipulated *not* by pilot *or* copilot but by both, working together. It would be difficult to learn, and if they were not able to do it, the plane would crash. But if they were able to do it, they could fly whenever and wherever they pleased." I could see in faces of the audience the impact of my pilot's metaphor, and when they rose to applaud, some in tears, I realized the times were indeed changing.

But not as fast as some people thought, because when I gave that same speech to the "spouses," mostly wives, at a large gathering of Iowa businesspeople, several tables of people left the room, and at the end I received barely polite applause. It was my first glimpse of the threat some women felt about the women's movement.

Nonetheless, things changed for women in my department. By 1980, all department heads were women, as well as the managing editor. In the sales and marketing and publishing management side of the business in 1979, there were two women advertising salespeople. Within five years, women were in the majority in those jobs, plus there were women advertising directors, publishers, and senior publishing executives. Not that I was responsible for all this change in women's status. The company itself became more assertive in hiring and promoting women, and the publishing and advertising industries became more open. (In fact, it is fair to say that now women hold dominant positions in both of those industries.) But I am proud of my small part in changing the workplace for women in our profession.

In addition, the secretaries and clerical workers in our company began to be accorded a more professional status, with investment in training and education, access to more benefits, and so on. And although I know that there are vestiges of the old paradigm still today, with secretaries making coffee and running errands, I believe the good companies and the good bosses have abandoned all that as a relic of the past. There are new struggles, to be sure, and there is a long way to go—particularly in the face of

Confessions of an Accidental Businessman

impending legislative changes—but there is no way to stop the momentum.

As for me, I now speak and conduct workshops for many different industries, and in probably a majority of these engagements, I am hired by, and am working for, a woman.

In my personal life, I became a fully rehabilitated sexist by the late seventies. I have learned and have benefited from the patience and wisdom of women whose friendship I treasure and will always try to nurture. And although I still sometimes struggle with the residual vestiges of testosterone poisoning and still appreciate the physical beauty of women, my true definition of beauty has changed a lot . . . .

❧ Romantic Revelations

My friend has an infallible rule
for spotting a romance in the office,
a rule true and proven over the years.
He calls it the Law of Romantic Revelation,
and it goes like this:
    If you think they're doing it,
    they're doing it.
Sounds silly but it's damn near perfect
if you have any power of observation at all.
If for instance a very solid citizen,
say a forty-five-year-old guy,
stops getting a haircut every other week,
and as the hair begins to hide his ears and collar,
you notice the gray ones are gone,
or if he shows up in an Italian blazer,
unvented,
with notched lapels,
watch out.
Next thing you know he's collecting wine
or original prints.
Then one day you're in a meeting
on personnel policy
and find he has become a feminist
since the last meeting,
or you notice in the corner of his office
a new Land's End canvas bag
for his running shoes and designer sweats
and one of those Fit at Fifty
posters on the wall.
You have but to keep your eyes open
and the object of his affectations
will come into focus
and the Law of Romantic Revelation
will unveil its infallibility once again.

Chapter Eight

In Which It Becomes Clear That Business Ethics Often Has Strange Definitions

New Orleans. Sin City. A notorious and mythical place in my southern childhood. In the fifties, every high school boy in the South dreamed of going to New Orleans where we would hear great jazz, meet great women, and escape all the prudish parental constraints under which we had to live our daily lives.

Finally, in college, I made it to the Crescent City, courtesy of the University of Mississippi marching band. Our football team went to the Sugar Bowl and the band got to follow. We rode on the City of New Orleans and within one hour of arrival were in the French Quarter, a place where anyone could get a drink at any time of the day or night, twenty-four hours a day, seven days a week. It is said that New Orleans has the highest per capita consumption of bourbon, Coca-Cola, and aspirin of any city in America. Crowds of drinking students and football fans filled Bourbon Street, stopping to yell football cheers, gawking into the open doors of the strip bars while a barker urged them with knowing winks to come in for the best part of the show. Dixieland music seemed everywhere, coming from every door, and black kids tap-danced on the corners for nickels and dimes. I made my way to Pat O'Brien's where, I had been told, I was to have a hurricane. Although I did not get to live out all of my high school fantasies about New Orleans, particularly the part about meeting great women, still all of those impressions—music, lights, half-naked women, and endless food and drink—seemed just wonderful to my college-boy eyes.

These were the images of New Orleans I carried into my adult life, but when I became editor and publisher of *New Orleans Magazine* in 1967, it was not that aspect of the city I expected to be a part of. No, I expected that I would become a media heavy in this glamorous and mystical city, that I would associate with the fun-loving social movers and shakers in the "City That Care Forgot." Not only that, I would be back in grassroots journalism, part of the new and burgeoning field of city magazine publishing.

Heed the Early Warning Signals

Every difficult job situation has its early warning signs, so two experiences in the first two weeks should have set me straight from the beginning.

When I first arrived, my new boss had arranged for me to be invited to the Mardi Gras ball of one of the secret societies, the "Krewe" of something or another. It was to be white tie and tails, a get-up I had never worn before.

The "ball" turned out to be a pageant acted by members of the Krewe, some of whom were deadly serious about it and others of whom were dead drunk, or on the way. The guests watched all this from bleachers, something like a sports event. After the pageant, members of the Krewe then "called out" from the crowd the ladies with whom they deigned to dance. Apparently, being "called out" was considered an honor; apparently also, to attend the ball and not be "called out" was something of a come-down. My boss graciously had arranged for my wife to be "called out" so that she might not feel left out of the festivities.

That was about all there was to the ball. White tie and tails, sitting in bleachers watching a corny pageant, then watching other people dance. It was more symbolic of what I was to be up against with the old money New Orleans society than I could have imagined at the time.

The second warning sign should have come when my new boss showed me the assigned parking places for the staff. Several of them were in "No Parking" zones on the street in front of our offices.

"How can these be assigned parking places?" I asked.

"That's the way it works here," he said. "We rent the places from the cop on the beat. If someone else parks in our place, he gets a ticket."

"And you pay the policeman?"

"Yeah. It's a way to supplement his pay. He also keeps an eye out for thieves. It's a double good deal for us."

"But illegal, right?"

"In New Orleans, it's not exactly illegal. We do things differently here."

Now just imagine this dedicated grassroots journalist's first impressions: a phony-baloney, pretentious social scene on the one hand and crooked payoffs on the other.

Caught in the Capital Crunch

Yet the New Orleans experience was destined to teach me some of the most valuable business lessons of my magazine career. Unfortunately, most of those lessons had to be learned the hard way.

The first shock was the financial condition of the magazine. Several New Orleans businessmen had capitalized the magazine a year earlier, but the founding publisher had badly underestimated the cost of producing a high-quality, slick, full-color magazine. With start-up costs and only five issues published, the operation was out of money and, in fact, was in debt to the printer who, fortunately for me, was also the principal owner of the magazine and thus had little choice but to extend the magazine's credit.

My first big assignment was to meet individually with the investors and convince them that I had the professionalism and know-how to make the magazine a success, then ask them for a further investment, enough to publish six more issues.

Shock number two came when I learned that the chamber of commerce, which was the official sponsor of the magazine by virtue of having given all the chamber members a subscription, had given those charter subscriptions for only the first six months. They were coming to an end, and there had been no effort to renew the subscriptions.

The implications of this were simple and disastrous: (1) We would have to continue the subscriptions at no charge until we could get the readers to renew (if we could). A burdensome cost item, but without reaching the readers, we had no product to sell the advertisers. (2) A heavy investment in subscription promotion. More cost.

I had no choice but to cut the size of the staff, reduce editorial and production costs, and still try to publish a magazine that readers would want to pay money for.

As managing editor of a major national magazine, I had lived in a relatively sheltered environment in that my concerns were editorial and only editorial. Now I found editorial to be the least of my worries. I had given up a good job with a substantial company to follow my dream of city journalism only to find that I had to be money raiser, circulation manager, advertising salesman, coffee maker, and floor sweeper, as well as editor.

To make matters worse, I had persuaded my friend George Bacon to join me as art director, a job in which he not only designed the magazine but did paste-up and all the mundane mechanical things he had been able to delegate to others at *Better Homes and Gardens.*

The investor calls went okay and we were able to get an infusion of money. But there was not time or money to do subscription mailings, so I resorted to telephone sales. This is not only expensive, with the majority of the revenue going to the telephone solicitors, but it also often makes people angry. Nonetheless, it was effective for several months, and as long as it was working, I could concentrate on other things.

Like advertising sales. A lot of our advertisers were also members of the chamber of commerce, thus many of them were now being solicited for subscriptions by our telephone salespeople. Some of the advertising managers were among those made angry by being interrupted at work to listen to a pitch for *New Orleans Magazine.*

Here's how an ad sales call would go:

"Hello, Mr._____, I'm Jim Autry of *New Orleans Magazine,* and I'd like to describe to you some of the advantages of advertising in this exciting new medium. . . . "

"I've heard of the magazine, Mr. Autry. What's the idea of having your people call me out of a meeting to sell me a subscription? I thought we got subscriptions compliments of the chamber."

"Well that was only for the first six-month introductory period. Now if you want to continue, you have to subscribe."

"If it's sponsored by the chamber, and I'm a chamber member, I should get it free."

"Of course, Mr. _____, all our advertisers will automatically be on the comp list, so yours would be free."

And so on. I must have had some version of that conversation at least fifty times. What I needed most in the world was a good advertising director.

The Importance of the Right Person
at the Right Time

At the time, Stanley Baron was selling printing. He wanted to work for the magazine, so the printer and I worked it out. Stanley was a one-man miracle. He was well known around town, a local boy, a musician, a *bon vivant* and raconteur, and a hell of a salesman.

We commissioned a reader research study, documenting the quality of our audience, then Stanley put together a presentation, and he was on his way. Despite resistance from the newspaper who, for reasons I could not fathom, considered us a threat, the ads began to come in.

But it was very difficult, and the city of New Orleans itself turned out to be a somewhat bizarre place to do business. Everyone, it seemed, wanted to instruct me about "how New Orleans works." I learned that there were the old families and the old money but not to confuse the two because the old families did not necessarily have money though some of them did, and when they did, it was old money.

Then there was the new money, a lot of which was oil money, New Orleans being second only to Houston, Texas, as an oil city at that time. The people with the new money probably had more than the people with the old money, but money did not guarantee acceptance by the old families.

Finally, I was told that there was the mob money and that the less I learned about that the better.

The challenge for the magazine, of course, was to walk a narrow line both in editorial coverage and in the ways we did business. We had to know not only the advertising people on whom we should call but also the less visible people in those businesses.

And then there were the shocks about "how business is done" in New Orleans.

I was having a great deal of difficulty persuading one

Confessions of an Accidental Businessman

small advertising agency owner to even let me call on him, much less to buy advertising in the magazine. One of my staff members suggested I talk with a very prominent, old-money businessman who liked the magazine and the idea of it and was one of the advertising man's friends who had helped the agency get started. I got an appointment.

"Mr. _____," I said, "I appreciate your seeing me. I will not presume to ask you to make a call for me, but I just want to ask your advice about how I might approach Mr. _____."

He thought a minute then said, "Well, I know that Bob has an eye for women. Why don't you try just having a cooperative woman call on him."

"Sir?" I asked. I was truly shocked, not only at the suggestion but at who was making it. I thanked him and left. I was not exactly a prude, but I don't believe I could ever have resorted to sexual payoffs in order to get business. So I never "put a woman" on Mr._____—and, I might add, I never got to call on him and he never bought an ad.

Making Sales and Cutting Costs

But as our salespeople learned the marketplace, and as Stanley Baron took our presentation around to the solid and straightforward advertising people in town, we began to book enough advertising to give our remaining staff a sense of momentum and a lift in morale.

I had laid off several people, including the managing editor. I laugh now remembering that I also suspended the contract writing and photography services of Bill Diehl who, several years later, became famous as the author of *Sharkey's Machine*, *Chameleon* and other best-selling novels.

The layoffs were very difficult for me. The staff was young, the people had come to the magazine with great enthusiasm and optimism, and considering the careers they might have had, they were not very well paid. They understood the situation, of course; it's just that each thought someone else should be laid off. It was a lesson in how essential people see their own jobs to be and how inessential they see other people's jobs to be.

Another lesson came in watching all of them go on to better jobs and better situations, although most of them had to leave New Orleans. There was comfort in seeing them succeed but disappointment in knowing I had lost them from my staff and that they would probably always hold it against me.

One Person's Journalism Is Another Person's Trash

Once the advertising and circulation crises were on the way toward being resolved, I turned my attention back to my first love, editorial. I had not gotten off to the greatest start simply because I had decided to given prominent coverage to the Garrison investigation.

I had arrived just as Jim Garrison, then district attorney in New Orleans, had launched his investigation into the "New Orleans connection" to the assassination of John F. Kennedy. Press people from all over the world flooded New Orleans as Garrison announced one finding after another, then announced he was about to make an arrest.

In the April 1967 issue, I put Garrison's portrait on the cover. My colleague Mickey Sheehan, who was called executive editor, had made a connection with a local writer who apparently was close to Garrison. It was something of a coup for us because this writer had an abiding antipathy toward the local newspapers. And he worked within our budget, which is to say, cheap. Like several writers and photographers in town, he regarded our magazine as a quality showplace for his work.

One might think that our coverage of Garrison would have been well received. To the contrary; people at the cham-

Confessions of an Accidental Businessman

ber of commerce, in advertising agencies, and in the various clubs and restaurants where my boss regularly ate, complained bitterly that I was giving some sort of endorsement to Garrison's investigation which they, particularly the old-money people, thought was just political grandstanding.

I countered that this was the biggest news story in the country and one of the biggest in the world at that time and that *New Orleans Magazine* would be thought thoroughly second-rate to ignore it. To his credit, my boss, who was under considerable social pressure and under considerable financial pressure because of the magazine, did not force me to abandon the story.

So after our initial stories, we followed it closely, then ran follow-up stories in the fall. Meanwhile, I had begun to meet with Garrison himself from time to time and became convinced he was onto something. Regardless of my feeling, there was very little else to publish about it, so I let it fade away.

Even during the time we were publishing the Garrison stories, however, we did not abandon our responsibilities to present a balanced profile of the community. We began to do more stories in which we celebrated the city: features on local hostesses, on houses, on churches, on the new NFL team the Saints, on businesspeople, and so on. We then did a special issue on oil and its impact on New Orleans, including an artist's rendering of the New Orleans skyline as it would appear with only the buildings in which some aspect of the oil industry was located. It was impressive.

We "presold" the issue, which means we went to leaders in the oil industry and told them that this was a salute to their industry in which we were sure they would want to advertise.

Indeed they did, and the October 1967 issue became the first profitable issue in the magazine's one-year life. At the same time, it was one of the best-read issues we had published.

Of course, the young journalists on the staff, plus other journalists in town, felt that I had sold out by preselling the issue and that I had abandoned real journalism by publishing all those soft features. It was another lesson for me: Sometimes there is a great gap between what the staff wants to produce and what the customers want to buy; and if I wanted to stay in business, I had best respond to the desires of the customers.

This is true in every business, of course, and it is particularly difficult for a manager when the workers feel he or she is "selling out" the quality of the product, regardless of what the product is.

The future of *New Orleans Magazine* became brighter that fall, even though the debt was still heavy and the pressure was still severe. We had proved a lot and I was feeling good.

Still, a lot was lacking. The whole enterprise seemed to me more like running a small retail establishment and less like being in the magazine business. Shades of Humboldt, Tennessee, and *The Courier-Chronicle*!

And once again, fate struck. I received a call from Chuck Coffin at Meredith Corporation. He explained that the company was starting a new division, special-interest publications, of which he had been named publisher, and he wondered if I would like to interview for the job of editorial director. He offered to come to New Orleans. Within a few days, we were eating crawfish bisque at the Bon Ton Restaurant and talking about the job.

A few days later, Bob Burnett, who at the time was general manager of the magazine division, called and said he'd like to visit. This time we went for boiled crabs to Fitzgerald's on Pontchartrain Lake. I had made up my mind to take the job before Bob arrived, and it took only about ten seconds for me to tell him I was interested. I told him I wanted to take George Bacon back to Meredith with me.

"I can't offer that, at least not now," Bob said.

Another Moral Dilemma

To accept the job meant I would be leaving George Bacon behind. In a very significant way, George had put his fate into my hands when he left *Better Homes and Gardens*. He had depended on me to turn *New Orleans Magazine* around and to guide it into such success that we would then be able to do other publications. It was to be fun, a kick, to live and work in New Orleans, putting out the city's only slick, full-color magazine. And it had been fun in many ways, but the business itself had given us plenty of agony. George was not only a person of great magazine design talent but he was inventive and whimsical in his own art, and he had quickly earned a place in the local community of artists.

I knew he would do well in New Orleans, regardless of whatever happened; still, it was a moral dilemma of major proportions for me. We talked about my leaving. I told him that if I took the job, I wanted, if at all possible, to make a place for him back at Meredith. I offered not to go, hoping really that he would take the decision off my back one way or another. I wanted him to say, "Hell no, you made me a promise, and you're obligated to stay here and see it through," or "Listen, I love it here and things will be fine. You should go." He was too mature for either of those. He wished me good luck whatever I decided.

So I told Bob Burnett yes. I was to examine many times in the next year whether or not I committed some form of betrayal, whether I sought only my own success at the expense of someone else. Even as things went well, I still felt I had somehow abdicated my responsibility to him.

As it turned out, George was made editor of *New Orleans Magazine*; then, after a couple of years, he left the magazine business forever and opened The Idea Factory in the French Quarter, selling his own art objects and wood products. He ran the shop with his wife Peggy until 1994, when he died of Parkinson's Disease. I was not able in those early years to make a place for him back at Meredith, though I suspect he came to love New Orleans so much he would not have returned to Des Moines. Yet today it nags at me that George died without my ever really knowing whether he felt betrayed.

Trading Small Business Ideas for Big Business Resources

As for me, the young journalist's fascination with grassroots journalism had given way to a more substantial interest in the *business* of journalism. I understood finally that journalism, by definition, is commerce, whether the big-time journalism folks want to talk about it or not, and I was ready to explore those possibilities. I also was ready to do so in an environment of resources and support, in a place where a good idea could get funded. Certainly I felt the excitement that comes from making something out of nothing, from pulling a good product out of the fire, from seeing the results of my own enthusiasm and optimism and hard work—but these experiences had made me realize that if I were ever to have the entrepreneurial thrill of starting a lot of new products, it would require more financial resources than I would be able to scare up on my own, particularly in New Orleans.

So not only was I ready to return to Des Moines, I was ready to cast my lot in life as a corporate man.

❧ Genealogy

You are
in these hills
who you were and who you will become
and not just who you are

> *She was a McKinstry*
> *and his mother was a Smith*

And the listeners nod
at what the combination will produce
those generations to come
of thievery or honesty
of heathens or Christians
of slovenly men or working

> *'Course her mother was a Sprayberry*

And the new name rises
to the shaking of heads
the tightening of lips
the widening of eyes

> *And his daddy's mother was a McIlhenney*

Oh God a McIlhenncy
and silence prays for the unborn children
those little McKinstry Smith Sprayberry McIlhenneys

> *Her daddy was no count and her daddy's daddy was no count*

Old Brother Jim Goff said it
when Mary Allen was pregnant

> *Might's well send that chile*
> *to the penitentiary soons he's born*
> *gonna end up there anyway*

But that lineage could also excuse
the transgressions to come

>   *'Course, what do you expect*
>   *his granddaddy was a Wilkins*

or

>   *The Whitsells are a little crazy*
>   *but they generally don't beat up nobody outside the family*

or

>   *You can't expect much work out of a Latham*
>   *but they won't steal from you*

In other times and other places
there are new families and new names

>   *He's ex P&G*
>   *out of Benton and Bowles*
>   *and was brand management with Colgate*

And listeners sip Dewar's and soda or puff New True Lights
and know how people will do things
they are expected to do
New fathers spring up and new sons and grandsons
always in jeopardy of leaving the family

>   *Watch young Dillard*
>   *if he can work for Burton he's golden*
>   *but he could be out tomorrow*

And new marriages are bartered for old-fashioned reasons

>   *If you want a direct marketing guy*
>   *get a headhunter after someone at Time, Inc.*

Through it all
communities new and old watch and judge and make sure
the names are in order
and everyone understands.

Chapter Nine

Death Among Us

If death is bad, impending death is worse. Death is always impending, of course, ours and everyone else's; but what I'm talking about is the obvious, imposing, intrusive impending death that begins with the news of cancer or AIDS then dwells among us at the office every day as we watch, though we try not to, a friend or colleague lose weight and lose hair, then lose finally the look that lets us know he is still trying to "beat this thing," as he told himself and the rest of us he would do those months ago.

I do not suggest there is a good way to die, but if I have my choice, I choose sudden death. Let it happen, as it did to one colleague, on the golf course while he was about to chip onto the green. He looked up from his eight iron, said, "I don't feel so good," then fell over and was dead by the time they got him to the hospital. Or another colleague who, succumbing to a brain aneurism no one knew he had, simply laid his head on the desk, as if taking a little rest, and was found by co-workers some time later.

But let it not happen, as it did for a close friend and

employee of mine, who said, "Jim, I know I can beat this thing, but I need to keep working." So he kept working, in and out of the hospital, until that day during a big strategic planning meeting, my secretary slipped me a note: "Red's failing fast; they want you at the hospital." He was the first person I ever watched die the last breath, even though at the time I knew I had been watching him die for a long time.

Business doesn't prepare us for the presence of death at the office. The business schools don't teach anything about it, about what the manager says when someone says, "I have cancer," or about what to say to the other employees who will have to spend days and days with this constant reminder of their own mortality.

It's different in the air force. Right at the beginning of pilot training, some instructor makes it his business to say, "Chances are some of you are going to get killed in this process of learning to fly." Not that I wasn't shocked our first night of night flying when a fellow student pilot named Ewing and his instructor went in, almost straight down, their crash lighting up the Arizona desert with a plume of fire the rest of us could see from the farthest point of our practice area. And not that there was not pain and tension as each plane landed and the dispatch clerk said, "Apache four two is in . . . Apache one-five is in," and so on until finally one number did not come in and we knew at last who it was.

Several pilots were killed during my first couple of years as a pilot, and it became clear that there were expectations it would happen and rituals for dealing with the deaths. Some of them involved flyovers in the "missing man" formation; others involved getting drunk and singing. And the one thing all of us did, as soon as possible, was fly again.

Beyond the rituals were the personal ways we had of expressing our grief, though I'm not sure we would have called it that. I remember the death of a fellow squadron member named Bradshaw who, as it happened, was killed flying in my place the plane I had been originally scheduled to fly. His engine failed on takeoff and when he touched back down on the runway and deployed his drag chute, it also failed, probably because he was going too fast. At the time, there was a lot of repair work on the runways, and off the end of this particular runway was a large pile of sand and soil. Bradshaw's plane hit that pile and exploded.

Flying was cancelled immediately and those of us preparing to fly walked back from our planes to the ready room. All of us had seen the accident and no one was talking. I was wondering particularly how Gary Kelly, another squadron mate and Bradshaw's good friend, would be doing. I spotted Kelly sitting on a stack of equipment staring out toward where the black smoke continued to rise from the wreckage. He had an unlit cigar in his mouth. He squinted his eyes, rolled the cigar a couple of times, then pulled it from his mouth and said, "Old Brad hit that sandpile going like a streak of shit, didn't he?"

I think it was Kelly's way of saying, "I loved Brad and I'm going to miss him." I have thought many times since of the strange ways men grieve, but on that day I could not have been more moved had Kelly been sobbing.

Perhaps what made death among us so different in the air force as opposed to in business was the understanding that it was all in the line of duty, an understanding that was honored by our official rituals.

Business Needs Rituals About Dying

Perhaps we should develop the same understanding in business. Couldn't sickness or death be thought of as "in the line of duty," something that happens as we go about our work— and sometimes even because of our work? In business, though, it is as if we never expect to have to deal with death among us until the funeral or memorial service. And there certainly is no honor in dying. There are no guidelines, no rituals; so, as with so many things involving the emotional and the spiritual, we are left in business to deal with death in our own individual ways. Some of us are more successful than others.

In 1960, when my younger brother died at the age of seventeen, I had been in my new copy editor job at Meredith only two months and was almost embarrassed to ask for time off for the funeral. When I did, my boss asked me when I expected to be back at work. At the time, I was not offended; I had no basis for comparing how a boss should react to the death of an employee's loved one.

The boss, of course, had to keep the work flowing. Business goes on, after all. I was still to discover that, even when an employee died and the rest of us were excused to attend the service, there was a good deal of logistical scurrying about covering the phones and keeping the work flowing.

It was in realizing that business goes on, despite everything, that I developed the understanding about some of the paradoxes of management and began to develop some thoughts about dealing with these paradoxes. When it comes to death, the manager has no choice but to recognize, honor, and support the expressions of grief and loss, but also no choice but to make sure the work keeps flowing.

This is not as simple as it seems and, poorly done, can make people feel that the manager and the company just don't give a damn that someone has died.

I'm not sure I ever got it right, because I'm not sure there is a right way to send these two messages: "I care about your loss and your feelings. Let's make sure the work gets done." Perhaps it is within those two realities that the whole core of conflict between the functional and the emotional exists in business. The manager is simply stuck with the fact that he or she does not have the luxury of the "either/or" world but must operate within the daily demands—both positive and negative—of a "both/and" world.

Managers Need Wisdom and Courage

This conflict is even more intense when dealing with an employee who wants to keep working while struggling with a terminal illness, and frankly I have never known a seriously ill person who did not want to keep working. I know of no one who said, "Well, I have a terminal illness so now I'm going to take advantage of all the support systems and all the disability payments and the medical leave and just stop working and enjoy life as much as possible until I die."

This is not the way people engage their lives; it is not the way they engage their work; and it is not the way they engage the certainty of their death. *I believe there is no stronger affirmation of the meaning of work in people's lives than the intense desire of dying people to keep working.*

How does the manager support that person while still making sure the work gets done? Beyond that, how does the manager honor and recognize that the presence of this struggle every day in the workplace is just terrible for everyone else's morale? There just are no absolutes in determining how to lead people through these situations. Sometimes I think that business educators believe that if a management problem can't be charted or graphed or analyzed and a solution put forth as a procedure or process, then the problem is not really a *business* problem. Any manager with real life experience knows, however, that the most challenging situations require our wisdom, not our knowledge.

After years of trying to figure it out, I decided that if managers are going to err, it should be on the side of compassion for the dying person. After all, if it is true that we need work to help define our lives and give them meaning, then work must have some part in helping and supporting us as the end of life comes. Of course, this requires enormous courage because of the technicalities and legalities of sick leaves, disability leaves, compensation issues, and other organizational concerns. It requires that managers insist that the system work *for*, and not against, the dying employee.

If, as a manager, you find yourself with a terminally ill employee, what you must do is recognize and embrace the paradoxes, support all the people, with special emphasis on the dying person, then follow your heart: look inward, look toward your faith, and do only what seems right.

This chapter is dedicated to the memory of George Bacon, Elizabeth Craster, Ron Davis, Bert Dieter, Bev Garrett, David Malena, Bill McReynolds, Wayne Miller, Jim Riggs, Noel "Red" Seney, and Betty Wood, all of whom died before their work was done.

✑ Death Message

I was in the big strategic planning meeting,
of all places,
the once-a-year-pull-out-all-the-stops-
and-try-to-convince-everyone-including-ourselves-
that-we-know-what-tomorrow-will-bring-
and-if-it-brings-something-different-
we-will-be-ready meeting,
when my secretary, eyes down and head shaking,
handed me the note:
"They want you at the hospital . . . Red's failing fast."

It does not work to say
that we are all dying
and it is simply a question of when;
it does not make death more natural
nor does it make us less surprised
even when we are expecting it.

"Any day now," we had been saying,
yet it seemed to me Red's last prank,
dying in the middle
of a strategic planning meeting,
knowing I would pick up and leave
and the planning department's beautiful schedule
would be forever out of whack
because death is just not a contingency
they know how to plan for.

His lung had collapsed by the time I arrived
but over the respirator mask
his eyes widened and he squeezed my hand
with more strength than he could spare.
His brother-in-law said,
"Hell, he's gone, he's not here now"

even though the breathing had not stopped.
And I thought of meetings and trips and parties,
of where he started and how far he came
from a tiny town in Iowa to a big publishing company
and how much he brought with him,
old-fashioned stuff and corny as hell,
yet something we all came to depend on
and would never be able to replace.

The next morning on my desk,
another note from my secretary:
"They finished the meeting without you."
And I thought,
it won't be the last time.

↬ Messages from Somewhere Else

It was during that long wailing ambulance ride to Memphis
after the heart attack
she dreamed about her brothers,
killed those forty years ago
working on the railroad.
Not dreamed about them exactly
but about looking at their pictures,
studying those young and arrogant railroad man faces,
then noticing another picture frame,
empty and blank saved for her,
a sign it was not yet time for her to go,
so, she told me later, she relaxed and enjoyed the trip.
Meanwhile trying to keep up with the ambulance
in my rental car
I heard the urgent whistle of a train
and looked to see it running parallel with the highway,
staying even with us.
Painted on the side of the freight cars
was some kind of slogan,
only an advertising slogan I'm sure,
stretched along the train,
car after car,
saying simply
We're pulling for you
We're pulling for you
We're pulling for you . . .

Chapter Ten

The First Taste of "Intrapreneuring"

One of my residual anxieties since childhood has been the fear that someone would judge me a quitter; so after I accepted the offer to return to Meredith, I began to fret that my former colleagues would think I was returning with my tail between my legs, that I couldn't make it once I was away from the protective culture of the Meredith civil service.

It became important then to see myself as returning in triumph—more important, in fact, than money. I agreed to a salary of $17,000 a year, four thousand more than I had been paid as managing editor of *Better Homes and Gardens* and only one thousand more than my salary in New Orleans. However, I did nothing to dissuade anyone's speculation that I had been lured back for big bucks.

Also, I talked about how exciting New Orleans had been and how much we had done and how influential the magazine was in the city. I let it be known that my interest in returning was the opportunity to be an entrepreneur within the company, to establish a new operation, and to create new products. I really don't know what people's impressions were; all my big talk probably served only to massage my own ego through the transition.

The truth was, I was so damned glad to be back I could hardly contain my enthusiasm. And that enthusiasm turned into a burst of creative energy I had not experienced before. Two situations presented themselves at once, both containing opportunities and lessons that were to serve me well for the rest of my business career: (1) I inherited a staff that had been, for lack of a better word, overmanaged. (2) The company was truly committed to starting new products.

Eliminating the Bureaucratic Nonsense First

Until 1968, the special-interest publications at Meredith had been known as the "idea annuals," the annual collections of editorial material on one subject, such as gardening or remodeling or Christmas decorations, which were packaged in magazine format and distributed on the newsstands. Editors in the book division put these publications together, and advertising salesmen in the magazine division sold advertising in them. Revenues from newsstand sales accrued to the book group and revenues from ad sales accrued to the magazine group. Strange, to say the least.

Bob Burnett was given the mandate to bring this publications department into the magazine division, to set it up as a separate profit center, and to make it grow while also using the department as a research and development group for new magazines.

The creative part of that mandate was mine to execute, and I was to do it with a staff who had been regarded mainly as a bunch of clip-and-paste artists. It had not been long since I'd had to lay off staff members at *New Orleans Magazine*, and I feared I would have to do the same in this new job.

Could these people rise to the occasion? Could they meet the demands of a quick-on-the-feet new product group? Were they even creative enough to develop new products? Would they want to?

If as a manager you have not had the opportunity to lift the burden of nit-picking bureaucratic policies and procedures off the backs of good people and then stand back and watch them work, you have missed one of the most inspiring management experiences of all. Because that's all I had to do.

I was appalled by the myriad rules and regulations under which these folks had been operating, including dress codes, office neatness guidelines, and so on. In going through a file of staff memos, I came across a list of rules including such items as, "The urbane editor eschews the boyish, tousled hair look." (As Dave Barry would say, "I am not making this up.") I learned about this stuff the first week; then in the second week, I gathered the creative staff together and said, "We have a lot of work to do, and I don't think we have time to pay attention to all these rules. I sure as hell don't have time to make sure you pay attention to them. So from now on, let's concentrate on doing good work, and that's what I'll evaluate you on."

It was as if they thought I had been sent to lead them to the Promised Land. They were hard workers, they were talented, they were committed to doing good work, and they were willing to turn on a dime and do new things. They had what I came to recognize as the spiritual essence of people fully engaged with what they had chosen to do. What more could a manager ask?

When I took the group, it was producing six publications a year. Within two years, we were producing eighteen publications a year with more planned. In addition, several of our titles were to become quarterlies within two more years, and we started one new subscription magazine for the company.

How One Crazy Idea Became a Major Profit Center

In the midst of all this activity, I got a call one day from my counterpart on the business side, the advertising director, Dan Matthews. Dan was a wild idea man, a great salesman who had grown up in Georgia and had sold himself into a successful career. He had an idea.

It seems that one of his advertising customers in the do-it-yourself home improvement field needed a custom publication produced, one that he could put his company's name on and could distribute as a give-away through his company's own distribution network.

"We can do that," said Dan. "And we can make more net profit at it than we can from six ad pages."

"How so?" I asked, not needing any extraneous work to do and being wary of Dan's ideas until I had heard them through.

"We just pick up some of our material, put it together in a booklet, and let them put their name on it."

There were a million questions: copyright, photographer and writer rights, budgets, and deadlines. But I said, "Let's get together with them and talk it over."

We flew to Chicago and met with the ad agency. They were extraordinarily nice people with great respect for our company and its resources. So we made a deal in which I agreed to produce the booklet on a fairly tight schedule. The problem was I had nobody available to work on it; but I figured, what the hell, if worse came to worse, Dan and I could pull it together. We could clip and paste if we had to.

The best person for the job was my friend David Jordan—if he still considered himself my friend. David had left *Better Homes and Gardens* shortly after I did, and, after a stint as director of photography at Obata Studios in St. Louis, had gone out on his own as a writer and photographer.

There was a bit of bad blood between us because, when I left *Better Homes and Gardens*, David had wanted me to recommend him for the managing editor job. I did not recommend him alone, but as one of two people. Jim Riggs chose the other guy, and David felt I had betrayed our friendship.

Indeed, I am not now sure that I did not betray him. At the time, I satisfied myself that David would not really like the job. I reasoned that his individuality and his general disregard for the corporate ways of doing things would work against him, that he would end up unhappy, and perhaps end up offending his bosses who might then fire him. Or perhaps I just sensed that Riggs was more disposed to the other guy; thus I chose the easy way out and did not make a strong case for David.

My failing was in not discussing this openly and honestly with David. I could have laid it out, just as I saw it, pointed out what I thought would be tough adjustments for him, then asked him to consider whether he really wanted the job or just the position.

Even though my reasoning ultimately *may* have been correct, I have no way to be sure because, in effect, I made a decision for David without involving him in it. In embracing my rather elaborate rationale, I convinced myself I had done the right thing, and at the time I managed to convince myself that David's anger with me was misplaced and unfair. (In the intervening years, I've seen this syndrome a hundred times: A boss becomes defensive and feels somehow unfairly attacked if an employee or colleague does not accept a decision without protest, but instead advocates for another position or questions the boss' judgment.)

By the time I returned to Meredith, I very much wanted to have a way to work with him again and to renew our friendship, if possible.

To my surprise, he made the first move by writing to let me know he was interested in working on projects for Meredith. In his letter, he referred to "the late unpleasantness," the same phrase Winston Churchill had used to refer to World War II.

So I called David about the booklet job. He was, and still is, the best woodworker, home-improvement editor/writer in the country. He agreed to do the booklet.

It was one of those projects in which everything went well. We did it, on time and on budget. We delivered it and were paid, and a new business was born. The business was to become Meredith Publishing Services, a custom-publishing operation which now is a highly profitable multimillion-dollar operation for Meredith, employing dozens of people.

Born, as I like to think of it, right out of the hip pockets of Dan Matthews, David Jordan, and Jim Autry.

As MPS picked up steam, the same editors and designers who were so busily turning out the special-interest publications also put their energies into the custom publications.

Watch Out for Customers on an Ego Trip

The next MPS job did not go so well. Again, I called on David Jordan. We traveled east to meet with an agency, and the first thing the agency president said to us was, "Understand this. Around here we work by the golden rule. He who has the gold makes the rules." That alone should have been a warning, but it wasn't and I plunged ahead.

Whereas the Chicago agency people had respected our expertise and abilities, these agency people second-guessed us to death. They began to fancy themselves editors, nit-picking details they did not understand, their changes pushing us up against the deadline wall, and their last-minute revisions as the project was *on the presses* driving up production costs. Then they insisted we stick with our original bid. It was very frustrating, particularly as we were trying to establish a whole new business, but these guys were the customers.

I'm not sure we broke even on that job, but the agency wanted us to do it again the following year, so we raised the price substantially and did it. In effect, the longer term impact of the agency posturing and pressuring was that the agency's client—the ultimate customer, the one paying the final bill—ended up paying more than was necessary every year we did that job. I call that the price of an ego trip.

The Price of Accomplishment Is That You Are Asked to Accomplish Even More

Despite a few problem situations, things could not have been better for me professionally. I was happy, I was excited, I had a good staff, I was creating new products and new businesses, and I felt I was finally trusted by senior executives whom I admired. It was just as I was feeling on top of the business that I got a call from Bob Burnett, setting up an appointment in his office the following week.

I became worried immediately. Who knows what causes these anxieties, but whenever things are going well, I keep expecting the next shoe to drop, I keep expecting something to go wrong, I keep expecting loss. It's as if some switch trips and I think, "I'm happy, something bad must be about to happen."

I couldn't imagine what Bob wanted. I reviewed everything we'd done in the SIP department and I knew he was satisfied with our progress. Perhaps I'd been too aggressive, too pushy; perhaps I'd offended other people in the company. I did not exactly whip myself into a frenzy of worry, but I was glad when the day of the appointment came.

It was bad news and good news. I was to leave SIP where I had worked so joyfully; Bob was changing the magazine group organization and wanted me to take over the chief editor's job at *Better Homes and Gardens*. The magazine needed work, he felt, and he thought I could do the job.

It was a great honor as well as a formidable challenge to be named editor of one of the largest magazines in the world and the largest (and most carefully watched) profit center in the company. Exactly ten years before, I had come to Meredith as copy editor, the lowest position on the staff, and now I was being given the top chair. I knew the staff was fat and fragmented, more of them than the magazine needed, still acting like several separate departments rather than one magazine staff, populated with moody and tempearmental people, and largely unfocused. I knew what had to be done, and the odd thing was that for the first time in my business career, I hadn't the slightest doubt I could do it.

After the glow of the promotion announcement wore off, I faced the reality that this job wasn't going to be fun. Although I had feared I might have to fire some of the SIP people when I first arrived, the situation had turned out well. Now I *knew* I would have to cut the size of the *Better Homes and Gardens* staff. It was simply too large for the number of editorial pages available, resulting in too much in-fighting and competition for space. There also were some fundamental creative changes needed, which would mean cutting the space being given to some subject areas and expanding the space given to others. More staff changes.

The SIP experience had been something like riding in on a white horse and liberating the people, but to some of the *BH&G* staff, I knew I would appear more like the grim reaper—not exactly the self-image to which I aspired.

Telling the SIP staff was very difficult. I knew they feared a return to the old kick-ass management style even though I also knew that was not to be. Their new editorial director was to be another friend, Neil Kuehnl, who would be moving from my old spot of managing editor of *Better Homes*. As it turned out, Neil led them and the new custom publishing group to even greater accomplishments.

The SIP staff surprised me with a going-away/promotion party. It was the first time since I left my old fighter squadron in France that I had wanted to cry. But of course, it being still the early seventies, I didn't. There were songs and cards and a few joke gifts. The most telling and prophetic gift came from the design department. They had made a large plaster mold of a millstone on which they had cast words in relief then painted the whole thing gold. It sits on the floor in the corner of my home office yet today.

The words: "BH&G. The Golden Millstone."

Chapter Eleven

Are We Having Fun Yet?

There was always more talk in the corporate world about fun than I was used to. I was a typical product of a dualistic industrial age. Work was work and fun was fun, and although I knew people who had worked hard at having fun, I didn't know anyone who had worked to have fun on the job. And by my conditioning, if someone had fun at work, he was likely to be fired. The two were not supposed to mix.

So that attitude caused me to wonder what was going on when, in almost every meeting of managers or employees, Bob Burnett asked, "Are we having fun yet?" I had no idea what he meant, so I asked him one day to explain it to a group of us.

He put a gloss on it that boiled down to the attitudes we have about doing good work and the feelings we have when we accomplish that work. In other words, pride in a job well done was the equivalent of fun. Or in Bob's words, "Putting it all together and making it happen" was fun.

Well, it sure wasn't my definition of fun. For most of my

career, my connections between work and fun had to do with people and activities that were ancillary to the work itself—things like conferences and retreats, fancy dinners while traveling on the expense account, all the usual stuff. Not the work itself, but the perks.

So what about fun itself?

When I think about working on my Uncle Elond's farm in Mississippi in the hot sticky summers of my growing-up years, I remember with great pleasure and satisfaction the work itself. I remember chopping cotton with my cousins and working the garden and doing the chores. It was a quieter, simpler, more honest time. My child self remembers great gatherings and singings and dinners, along with the forbidden things: swimming at night and stealing watermelons and dancing on the river bridge to the music from someone's car radio. In fact, in that context, the work and the fun were inextricably connected. I don't believe we could have enjoyed all the social things had we not been celebrating the completion of good work, whether a day of it or a season of it.

It is that kind of fun—celebratory fun—that I think also had the most meaningful and intense connections with my jobs over the years.

The Big Barbecue Debate

Last year, I was one of the keynote speakers for Cox Communications at its big annual management conference in Phoenix. I had noticed on the roster that one of the top officers, David Easterly, was to be in attendance, giving me an opportunity for some of the kind of "corporate foolishness" I hadn't enjoyed in a while.

When I first heard of and corresponded with David, he was publisher of the Atlanta newspaper. I was visiting the city and, as I feel called by the Almighty to do, was checking out a local barbecue restaurant.

Anyway, I visited a place in Atlanta called The Texas State

Line where, on the bulletin board for all to see, was a letter from David Easterly, on his company letterhead, extolling the excellence of the establishment's barbecue. After trying the food for myself, I judged it good but not nearly good enough to warrant an endorsement of the extravagance of Mr. Easterly's.

At the time, I was vice president and general manager of magazines at Meredith, so I wrote to Easterly on my letterhead and set him straight, not only about his barbecue insensitivity but about barbecue generally. Mr. Easterly replied with a very ungracious letter purporting, as Texans will do, that the only real barbecue is beef. At the same time, allies at the Atlanta newspaper sent letters of support to me. They had to be circumspect, of course, as Easterly was their boss. The finale of this nonsense was the publication of all the letters and notes in several of the Cox newspapers, including ones in Georgia and Texas.

The fun of it was that two businessmen who had never met and did not know each other would laugh at themselves, would parody their own positions (including their big-time letterhead), would parody the "art" of business correspondence, and would parody the posturing of two executives engaged in serious negotiations. Some might call it a waste of time, but those are the folks who aren't having any fun at work. And these are the folks who may be taking themselves, and their fancy titles, too seriously. The point, of course, is to take our work seriously while not taking ourselves so seriously.

So, these fifteen years later, after my introduction as a keynote speaker to the Cox group, I expressed surprise that I would be asked because I noted that David Easterly is now president and chief operating officer, "despite his serious barbecue disability." I then told the story, which not only brought a note of hilarity to a serious morning but also, I suspect, put an even more human face on the president.

As for Easterly, he introduced himself after my speech and said, "You obviously know more about making a speech than about barbecue."

Who knows how long this will go on? For years, I hope.

The Great Golf Myth

One of the most widely held misconceptions about business-people, particularly men, is that they play golf to have fun. Fun is rarely on the agenda of a business golf outing. Mostly, it is about contacts and selling and politicking and maneuvering.

Golf is also about providing supposedly nonbusiness conversational opportunities for businesspeople. It is true that most businesspeople I've met have little to talk about except business and their current sport. Until the surge of tennis interest in the eighties, this sport was always golf.

I would meet a stranger at the Magazine Publishers of America conference, or some other industry meeting, and if he wanted to make some nonbusiness conversation, he would inevitably ask, "What's your handicap?"

If you are not a golfer and don't even know how the handicap system works—as I don't—this question might provoke several kinds of responses. I usually would mumble, "I'm not a golfer," then quickly say, "I play tennis," which was not a lie but also not entirely true, because the answer implies an intensity of interest I did not possess.

I might try to quip, "Oh, I'm usually handicapped at about seven to four odds."

The response I always wanted to give but never had the courage was, "Inadequate sexual apparatus." A couple of friends and I had a lot of fun dreaming up answers to the "handicap" question, but I never had a minute's fun playing golf.

I have been asked, in complete seriousness, "How did you get so far in corporate life without being a golfer?" It is a good question because there are companies in which people have suffered disadvantages for the lack of exposure and contact available through the playing of golf. (News stories noted last year that one of the first conversations about a Disney/ABC deal took place between Michael Eisner and Warren Buffett in a chance post-game meeting at an exclusive golf club.) My answer to that question, which may be closer to the truth than I want to admit, was that "Bob Burnett and Ted Meredith are not golfers."

Fun as an Escape from the Tension

The fun I remember most took several forms. Some of it was in reaction to the rules and regulations or the conditions of the workplace; some of it was an attempt to overcome tension between people or to find relief from the pressure of overwork.

In the early days at Meredith, there was no air conditioning, the building being a relic of an earlier kind of industrial architecture that did not accommodate air conditioning. Only two or three rooms in the whole place had it: the test kitchens and a couple of conference rooms. Obviously, this became a sore point during those hot and humid Iowa summers, which are so good for growing corn and so bad for working in a non-air-conditioned office.

The first reaction, of course, was to complain. The next reaction was to manufacture a reason to have a meeting in one of the air-conditioned conference rooms. This became such a problem that there was established a whole scheduling system for the conference rooms.

There were those rare occasions when the heat became so unbearable that management made the decision to send us home. Most of the time, however, we improvised. For lunch, we adjourned to a little place called "Lemmo's," where we had Italian sausage sandwiches and frosty mugs of beer. Many times, after the second mug, we concluded that we could hold a meeting at Lemmo's and be more productive than at the office. By the third mug, we no longer were hostile and anarchistic toward management and its intransigence about air conditioning the building; we were instead the most productive editorial group on earth.

Also in the early days, in the days when I could not afford restaurant lunches and my job in editorial did not justify taking anyone to lunch, I brought my lunch in a brown bag, much as I had in my younger school days. So did my friend David Jordan. At the time, it seemed a come-down, he from being a communications officer on a destroyer in the navy and I from being a jet-fighter pilot in the air force. All that competence and skill, we felt, and we could not afford to buy a restaurant lunch.

So we turned it into fun in the most childish of ways. The Meredith building was next to a bridge across the Raccoon River. Before lunch, David and I folded a dozen or so paper airplanes and paper boats. At lunchtime, we took our brown bags and crossed the river bridge, pausing to sail the airplanes down into the river. Then we ate our lunch in the park across the river and floated our paper boats. We'd take the boats upstream to launch, then run like hell downstream where we would have stashed a lot of rocks and dirt clods, with which we then blasted the boats as they floated by. In retrospect, it was childish, it littered, and it may have denoted deep psychological problems; but damn, it was fun, and somehow it diluted a lot of negative stuff for us.

Still, this was not fun on the job; this was fun as escape from the job. And it did not stop there. During winter, we took our airplanes to the cavernous photo studio where the planes became more sophisticated. Then David, a master woodworker, began to make boomerangs and other flying devices. Before we knew it, this foolishness evolved into competitions that took on a life of their own.

Later, the escape became more serious. As I rose in management, George Bacon and I felt the intense pressure of balancing the needs of the staff with the directives of our bosses. He and I and a couple of other people formed what we called our Thursday-afternoon-get-a-jump-on-the-weekend club. We even had our own emblem, which George designed and made into a miniature flag that we then hoisted at whatever bar we chose for the week's meeting. I was also supposed to write an anthem to sing before every meeting but I never got it done. It was fun and it was a pressure-reliever for George and me.

Fun as a Bond in the Community of Work

The people on the editorial and design staffs enjoyed working together and they enjoyed having fun together. That mixture served to bond us into a community in which we did good work while we supported one another personally. Oh, we would never have used this language to describe how we were and what we did, but we felt it.

On the surface, it sometimes was just silly as hell. Underneath, it meant a lot. At almost every social gathering, after the initial polite greetings, a predictable group of us would gather in some corner for the "Chinamen never eat chili" song. Red Seney was the leader. Another wonderful man, Ed Young, copy editor of *Successful Farming* magazine, was the resident philosopher. "Let us put aside the cares of the day and let mirth reign unrestrained," he would say. Then we would launch into "Aiy, aiy, aiy-aiy, Chinamen never eat chili. This is the first verse; it's worse than the last verse; so waltz us around again Willy." After that refrain, we'd point to someone who then had to come up with a limerick. The later the hour, the more obscene the limericks. But they were always clever and their cleverness, their turn of phrase, their rhyme scheme always overshadowed the obscenity. At least we thought so.

Many years later, I visited Red Seney in the hospital as he was approaching the end of his life, stricken by bone marrow cancer. "Hey, Autry," he said to me, "How about a round of 'Chinamen never eat chili'?" And we sang a verse, and I recited one of his favorite limericks:

> *There was a woman from Exeter*
> *Who was so beautiful men craned their necks-at-her.*
> *One went so far*
> *As to wave from his car*
> *The distinguishing mark of his sex-at-her.*

Don't ask me why that moment fifteen years ago in a

hospital in Des Moines brings me to tears as I write this, now on an airliner flying from Sydney, Australia, to San Francisco. It is something about death, of course, but I think it is also something about the bonding power of fun.

Fun in the Work Itself

I remember wash day in Mississippi when I was a child. We would take everything to be washed down to a special spot on the creek. There we'd find big black iron washpots that had been hauled by mule to that place perhaps years before. The men would build small, smoky fires to keep away the mosquitos and larger fires under the washpots. We'd carry buckets of water from the creek, and the washing would begin. It was an all-day affair, punctuated by lunch and naps and lots of playing in the water. Lord, how the women worked and sweated over those pots, always scolding us to stay back and not get burned.

But it was fun. Even in all that work, our mothers and aunts seemed to be having fun—seemed to be celebrating the doing of the work, the outdoors, the separation from the usual chores of the house itself.

At some point in my career, I began to understand that the power of fun and good times did not have to be about escape, about coping with the job, about finding psychic rewards on our own. There could be a lot of fun in the work itself.

The first example that pops to mind is a Christmas-issue editorial planning meeting. Because we worked so many months ahead of publication date, we found ourselves planning and putting together the December issue in the midst of a hot, sticky summer month. It was not a positive environment for creative thinking about holiday decorations and foods and entertaining—subjects that made up the bulk of the December issue.

Bringing fun and good humor to the problem, the main editor for the issue, Elizabeth Craster, surprised the editorial management group one year by turning the whole thing into a holiday reception. We opened the door to the conference room to find it completely decorated for Christmas with Liz dressed as if greeting friends at her home on December 15. We had to laugh. She served holiday snacks and played carols on her music system before settling down to the meeting.

It was fun, it changed the mood, and I believe it resulted in better editorial work on that year's December issue. The party became a tradition that was repeated for many years.

I also remember the fun of a photo shoot. There is just something about the hard work of traveling, often in the most primitive of circumstances, about getting locations and props, about coordinating people, about coaxing and cajoling a few smiles from a baby you plan to feature on the cover, about praying for sunshine for a garden shoot, about balancing the artistic temperaments. In the end, that "something" is fun, the sheer enjoyment of the doing and the enormous satisfaction of putting the finished transparencies on the viewer and picking the best.

I always loved the art of a well-done presentation. What fun to watch the faces of people nodding and responding to the points you are making. I still feel that today as I work with, and speak to, management groups.

I could feel the electricity when a group of advertising salespeople and managers returned from a major presentation, laughing, giving the high-fives, celebrating in those kid ways we learned on the playground years ago.

These things are what I believe Bob Burnett meant about the fun you get "when you have put it all together and made it happen."

Fun as a Management Tool

I came to understand also that fun and good times can be a powerful management tool. I realized that the point was not escape but celebration. We not only need dignity and worth and meaning from our work; we need celebration. A lot of managers kid themselves that conferences and retreats are about learning and goal-setting and planning for next year's accomplishments. These gatherings are about celebration: of one another, of what we have accomplished, and of what we do together. Oh yes, we might do some learning and goal-setting and planning while we're at it, but that is *not* what the conferences are about.

And part of that celebration is the sheer fact that the company is willing to spend all that money to celebrate people's work with a meeting in a nice warm and sunny place with a golf course and swimming and good food. I still know managers who feel those conferences are about hard work and planning. And I'm sure that's what the IRS thinks they *should* be about. But they're about fun and celebration.

I think all the off-site meetings of business groups have the potential for that kind of celebratory work, and I took it upon myself as a senior manager to ensure that those kinds of gatherings took place, even in tough economic times when such meetings seemed "discretionary" and not worth the expenditure. There were many senior managers who disagreed with me, who treated these conferences as rewards rather than as necessities—I think because they seemed too much like play and not work. But I always felt they were highly worthwhile investments in the community of people who, after all, were producing and selling the products that ensured our success as a company.

Nor should managers underestimate the value of small daily opportunities for fun and celebration. The personal ones—birthdays, babies, and so on—lift morale and make the *people themselves* feel celebrated. The professional ones—bell-ringer parties to honor a successful sale or the getting of a new customer or the beating of the monthly goal—also lift morale and make the people feel *their work* is celebrated. Still today, I tell managers everywhere to avoid the trap of feeling that these events are in any way a waste of time or money.

A Manager's Responsibility:
To Ensure the Enjoyment of Work

I also came to realize that the people themselves *will* use their pursuit of fun in one way or another, either as a protest, an escape from the pressures of work, or as a way to rejuvenate their commitment to work and the energy to do it.

I used to ask managers, "What are you doing to ensure that your people are enjoying this work as much as possible?" It was a serious business question, because if your people are not having fun, you are not making it as a manager and you likely are *taking yourself too seriously.* I truly believe that people will take their work more seriously if they are enjoying what they do and enjoying the community of people with whom they do it. In other words, they do better work if they are having fun. So see to it.

As for top manager/leaders, I'm not sure they get to have fun in exactly the same ways. It always seemed a shame that as a top corporate executive, I was disconnected from the everyday fun of the workplace. Occasionally, at some special event, I might wax nostalgically about the fun we had in the "old days," but it was always met, I suspect, with some amusement and perhaps disbelief. Finally I had to accept that my satisfaction was to come more from watching the fun (and making sure it was happening) than from participating in it myself.

Perhaps at that stage of the career, golf might have come in handy.

Chapter Twelve

Staying on Course and Making Big Changes—At the Same Time

The first thing you learn as editor of *Better Homes and Gardens* is that it is the largest profit center in the company, the goose that laid the golden egg, the mother magazine, the source of everything with the *BH&G* name attached, from special interest publications to the world's all-time best-selling cookbook—in many ways, *BH&G* is the foundation of the company. Which means that the second thing you learn is that everybody in the company, from the CEO on down, is watching every damned move you make.

The good news is that corporate management would always provide the resources needed to make a magazine worthy of all that attention. What corporate management could not necessarily provide, however, was the right staff at the right place at the right time. That was up to the editor, and when I became editor in 1970, I knew we did *not* have the people we needed at the right place at the right time, yet we were overstaffed in some areas. Still, there was a core of good, experienced editors with insight and judgment. My immediate job was to rebalance the staff and build a productive community of people.

Learning a Better Way
to Do Layoffs

First came the layoffs. How painful to let people go just because there was no place for them, and not enough pages for them to fill—plus there were creative and conceptual changes coming that would preclude them from ever having enough pages to fill.

At *New Orleans Magazine*, when I had to cut the size of the staff, I was completely without experience in layoffs and thought the best thing I could do was to be a friend, to commiserate, to blame the magazine's circumstances. In other words, I tried to make the process as painless as possible for myself while also convincing myself that the way I had chosen was less painful for the people losing their jobs.

This, of course, was patently ridiculous, and the experience became another of my defining moments as a manager: Despite taking them to lunch in the French Quarter or at our magazine's favorite restaurant, The Bon Ton, drinking Rum Ramseys and a bottle of Vouvray, getting a bit sloshed, and shaking my head and grimacing at the injustice of it, *the people still felt betrayed and still saw me as the instrument of that betrayal.*

It was not betrayal, but indeed I was the instrument of their misfortune, however that was to be described. What I learned was that I could not duck the responsibility for the tough work, and I could not try to dismiss my involvement in the decision or blame it on the great unseen forces of commerce.

So at *Better Homes and Gardens*, I was straightforward, blaming no one but myself for making the decisions that led to the elimination of the jobs. The people did not thank me for my straightforwardness, of course; some of them were angry, and others were devastated. It was painful as hell for me. I cursed the circumstances, I wanted to blame my predecessor who had hired people needlessly, but still I felt in the long run my honesty—both with the employees and with myself—would be worth the immediate pain.

The People Generally Know What to Do

I was sure I knew what needed to be done to get the magazine back on track. At the same time, I knew the staff had been working diligently and in good faith on the magazine as it was. I had thought I would have a staff meeting, tell them how I thought the magazine should be, and call on them to do it that way from now on. It was only through luck that I stumbled onto a better way.

I was having lunch with my old friend Red Seney, who was now once again my employee, and asked his general view of the magazine and what we should do. To my astonishment, he wanted to do exactly what I thought should be done. It had not occurred to me that this core of good, experienced editors also knew what to do—that I had not come upon a direction by any intrinsic genius but by good editorial judgment and common sense.

So I began a round of informal meetings, lunches mostly, with members of the staff, one at a time. It was a revelation. There was broad consensus on the magazine's errors and lack of direction as well as on what should be done. There were differences of style and detail, but no fundamental differences.

The next major area to be addressed was visual style, graphic design, photography, illustrations. This was the realm of the art director, and I knew this was probably to be the key hiring decision of my new job. The art director at the time had not been in the job very long and thus had not really had the chance to show what he could do with proper direction. The only problem was that he seemed universally disliked by the staff. Every editor I talked with, without exception, urged me to replace him.

Deciding What's Most Important:
Popularity or Talent

This was one of those common and difficult management dilemmas. Clearly I couldn't make such a key decision based on the popularity of the person; yet the art director is a highly visible and very influential force and must be able to inspire people visually and enlist their cooperation in many different ways, affecting how the magazine will look. How could he do that if he was so disliked?

I had worked with him in the past, I liked him, and I admired his talent. His personal style was regularly confrontational and even defensive from time to time. He was a superb athlete and, in his fairly overt physicality, he sometimes appeared threatening during a disagreement—even on a couple of occasions suggesting to a fellow staff member that they "step outside" to settle a disagreement. If he was to stay on the job, he would simply have to attend to some of this behavior and work at building more personal support.

His saving grace was that he was damned talented, he was a good teacher to the younger people, and he truly cared about his work and about the magazine.

So I talked with him and agreed that he would stay in the job. It proved to be a very good decision and a very valuable learning experience. His tenure was not without a running undertone of discontent; in fact, at times it seemed like one damned thing after another in the interpersonal relationships area. But as the magazine began to look better and as our newsstand sales and subscription renewals rose, even his active antagonists came to respect his work, if not his personal style. And at least he was actively working at building better relationships.

Although this situation taught me a good deal about evaluating people on the basis of their results and not their pop-

Confessions of an Accidental Businessman

ularity, it also demonstrated the absolute necessity for people in management positions to be the *first* to accommodate the other viewpoint. I began to think of this as a kind of management *noblesse oblige* without the snobbery.

As for my liking him, there were staff members who said, "You can afford to like him. You're his boss and he won't give you any shit." What they didn't know was that his edges were no less sharp with me.

This relationship also helped me understand how to put aside my macho competitiveness—the need to "win" arguments—and to simply concentrate on the *content* of the other side of the argument. This understanding served me well throughout my senior management career as I watched other top managers let themselves be drawn into some symbolic joust while their businesses suffered.

I believe the art director grew immensely from these experiences as well, because he went on to a fruitful and productive career in editorial management.

Facing the Threat of an Obsolete Product

As for the magazine itself, I had plenty of somewhat overbearing things to worry about. These were not easy years to be editor of *Better Homes and Gardens*. It was the time of social unrest, Vietnam War protests, and young people's outcry against business and crass commercialism—against owning homes and raising families and cutting the grass and having dinner parties—against anything, in other words, their parents had done. The problem was that their public visibility had a great impact on attitudes. When I visited college campuses in those days as a guest lecturer or to conduct workshops, the students were frequently hostile.

"How can you call yourself a journalist," they would ask, "when all you do is put out a glorified catalogue of your advertisers' products?" Or, "How can you create this medium of materialism and call it a good magazine?" These are the milder versions of what I faced on campus.

What I feared was that *Better Homes* could begin to look irrelevant in a world in which "relevancy" had become the clarion call of young people. I feared the magazine could become just a symbol of an American way of life that had seen its best years. I feared that these kids would indeed grow up, reject marriage and home ownership, reject the traditional American dream, and simply choose other options.

I feared this not only because of what it would do to magazines like mine but also because of what it would do to the country. Despite all my own concerns about the war and about civil rights, and despite my own disdain for mindless materialism, I certainly was not ready to reject the potential of home and family life as the best environment for raising children. Even though I was divorced and remarried by then, I still was damned sure the traditional environment, distorted and dysfunctional though it might sometimes be, was far better than the one I was raised in, by a single mother in an apartment. Sure, some single parents do well at it, and sure, a lot of broken home children of that era, including me, had turned out okay. I knew some of those folks, but I knew other people, high school and neighborhood friends, particularly from Lamar Terrace in Memphis, who had married too young and had children too young and who felt cheated. I knew others who went to prison.

How strange it was, coming from my particular upbringing, to feel myself becoming something of an arbiter and defender of family life, at least in the popular media. It had not been too many years before that I shared the superficial view of those college journalism students that magazines like *Better Homes and Gardens* were without substance, were just collections of pretty pictures for ladies who had little to worry about but this spring's window treatment and color scheme.

It had been a struggle for me to understand the nature

of the magazine and the nature of what I later came to call "positive materialism," which I defined as using things to enhance life and good family relationships rather than using things for status or upward mobility. I worried that perhaps my concept of "positive materialism" was simply a rationalization to convince myself that the journalism I had chosen was not frivolous. I came to believe in it sincerely, and I knew it had value in people's lives, but how could I engage this editorially and how could I engage the issues of positive family life in an atmosphere so seemingly hostile to those issues?

When in Doubt, Ask the Customers

I decided to turn directly to the *Better Homes and Gardens* readers themselves (rather than just their college-age children). Our staff, with the help of top scholars and other professionals, put a questionnaire into the magazine, entitled "What's happening to the American family?" We were overwhelmed with 320,000 responses. The results were an affirmation of family life in whatever form it took, and the magazine got quite a bit of attention by publishing a report on the research and sending a copy to every governor and to all members of Congress. When I was asked to appear on the "Today Show" and be interviewed by Barbara Walters, I was scared to death as well as star-struck.

The response meant two things to me: (1) These middle-class, home-owning American people were eager to be heard; and (2) I could give them that voice, and at the same time, redefine to some extent *Better Homes and Gardens'* mission as a magazine.

Our next major editorial effort was an award-winning series entitled, "Environment Yes, Hysteria No." In effect, we began to give our home and family magazine a more active editorial role in the world of our readers. And the readers liked it. Newsstand sales and subscription renewals moved steadily upward.

What to Do When You Resign,
Then Change Your Mind

Nonetheless, with all the magazine's success, I was having grave conflicts with my boss, the editorial director. We were not agreeing about covers or about staff or about editorial direction.

I did not handle this well. I did what I have advised perhaps a hundred people *not* to do. Having turned around an ailing magazine, I thought I deserved not to have to put up with all of this guy's petty crap; but rather than try to work through the conflicts directly with my boss, I went straight to his boss' boss, Bob Burnett, CEO of the company.

"Jim," he said, "I think he just wants more communication; he wants not to be left out of the loop."

"I think he wants to look over my shoulder and try to take credit for the magazine's current successes."

"Well, I don't want to intervene," Bob said. "Keep trying to work with him."

My ego was too much in the way for me to really try working with him, and in fact, I was pretty self-righteous about it. Why in the world should I accommodate this phoney management structure when I was doing what my boss had not been able to do? What was this all about? Indulgence, I concluded. Pure management indulgence.

What I chose *not* to do is what I was always encouraging my people *to* do in their own relationships: to find common ground, to realize that we are in this together, to understand that our own contributions are but a part of the greater work, some of which is not visible to us.

Things got no better. My boss kept pressing and I kept resisting, a situation that, along with my attitude about it, led to a crisis I had not expected.

One day, I received a call from John Mack Carter, an almost legendary figure in magazine publishing. He wanted to talk to me about taking over as editor-in-chief of *Ameri-*

can Home. The salary and perks were overwhelming: double my present salary plus a townhouse in New York plus all kinds of ego-boosting things like a car and driver, a paid trip anywhere in the world each year, and so on. Though I had spent a lot of time in New York, I had never fancied living there; but my wife, Dorothy, was a New Yorker and she was excited at the prospect of returning.

So, thinking only of "the situation" with my boss and allowing myself to feel unappreciated, I resigned as editor of *Better Homes and Gardens.*

This episode taught me so many lessons that I think of it as a seminal business experience.

I carefully wrote a letter of resignation and delivered it myself, not to my boss, the editorial director, but to the president of the magazine group, Wayne Miller. Wayne can best be described as a gentleman in the old-fashioned sense, before that term took on its paternal, sexist overtones. He was a decent and fair boss and a splendid, caring human being.

He said, "I don't want to accept this resignation, and I am asking you not to make a final decision until I talk with Burnett who is in New York."

"I've already told John Mack Carter that I'll take the job. That's already a commitment as far as I am concerned."

"I understand that," Wayne said, "but I'm asking you to hold out just the possibility of changing your mind until Bob gets here this afternoon. He's taking the Lear back and would like to see you at four o'clock. "

I did not expect this response and it made me uncomfortable. The decision itself was difficult enough without now having to defend it against a sales pitch by people I had come to respect deeply. I had made up my mind. Management had plenty of chances to rectify the conflict situation with my boss and it seemed too late to do anything now.

"I can't promise anything," I said, "but I'll meet with Bob."

Bob was still on his way from the airport when I showed up at his office. So I waited. I hadn't spent a lot of time there and I was impressed by the grandeur of it: sofa, carpeting, huge desk, paintings, sculpture, plaques and awards and photographs everywhere—in other words, everything I was to come to know as standard executive office accoutrements—plus his famous sign, "Are We Having Fun Yet?"

I was not having fun anticipating the meeting with Bob. I had assumed that my resignation would not create much of a stir, despite the success of the magazine. It had seemed to me that, over the years, Meredith's posture was to take comings and goings in stride, with no particular significance attached to any of them: the Meredith civil service syndrome. I just had not anticipated that Wayne Miller would refuse to accept the resignation or that Bob Burnett would care enough to fly back from New York on the Lear. On the one hand, I was flattered; on the other, I was scared to death. I did not want to face the big man himself as he tried to sell me into staying.

I heard Bob greeting his secretary in the outer office and her telling him I was waiting. He entered with all the cordiality, even affection, of a long-absent close friend. Then we sat on the big sofa and he was silent for what seemed a very long time.

Finally, looking me straight in the eye, he said, "I've been an asshole about this conflict you've been in," he said.

Imagine that. Imagine how shocked I was.

I tried to dissuade him. "No, Bob, it's not just about my conflict with my boss . . . " I had intended to say it was also about a big opportunity in New York, but Bob interrupted.

"Of course it is," he said. He was right, of course. "You've done a great job with *Better Homes*, and I already had some changes planned, but I ignored your situation too long."

He did not let me speak.

"For a while now," he continued, "we've planned (I noticed he used the editorial 'we') to make an organizational change that puts you in charge of all magazines and special

Confessions of an Accidental Businessman

interest publications. Your possible resignation (I noticed he used the word "possible" for something I thought was *fait accompli*) simply causes me to advance the timing of the plan."

He paused briefly but not long enough for me to point out that I had indeed resigned and had accepted another job.

"So effective tomorrow morning, we are promoting you to vice president and editorial director of the magazine group and increasing your salary by ten thousand dollars. Plus there will be other opportunities for salary growth."

Then he stopped, and I knew it was my turn to talk. Almost.

"I do want you to stay, Jim. You're one of my people, and you'll be spoiling a lot of big plans if you leave." There was an almost mysterious quality to the talk of "opportunities" and "big plans," but I trusted Bob to have something specific in mind that he did not want to reveal. And I was moved emotionally to be called one of "my people."

"Bob," I said, "I trust and admire you more than any businessperson I know. But I have resigned. I have accepted another job. I've given my word. John Mack Carter has a newspaper ad ready for the *New York Times* announcing my editorship of *American Home*. I also like and respect John, and I cannot let him down and I cannot go back on my word."

I knew Bob respected my feelings; I knew he also liked and respected John; but I knew he intended to talk me out of it.

Somehow he did. One of the things he said, which guides me still today, was, "Don't make long-term decisions for short-term reasons." And he said, "Look, John has been in this same position at least once in his career. I believe he'll understand and will accept your change of mind."

Understand that I was not changing my mind for money or perks or anything other than the pure desire to continue to work for Bob Burnett and to be involved in other magazines and new products. And it also had a lot to do with the absolute impossibility of saying no to Burnett. No wonder he had been the best advertising salesman in the business.

I agreed to stay, but I felt like hell. There was no joy or celebration in it. "I'll need to call John," I said, "as soon as possible."

"Do it from my house, then we'll have some wine and celebrate your promotion," he laughed.

John Mack Carter is widely regarded in the magazine business as one of a kind—a decent person, a supportive boss, and another gentleman in that old-fashioned sense. He deserves the reputation. I found him at home. He came to the phone with welcoming words, assuming that my call concerned something about my imminent move to his company.

"I have bad news," I said. He listened and said, "You're sure?"

"I am," I said, "and believe me, John, going back on what I told you is one of hardest things I've ever done. I feel like a traitor."

"It's okay," he said, "most of us who've been around the business a while have had a situation like this ourselves. I just hope you're making the right decision."

I am still grateful to John Mack for that graceful response. He went on to become the highly successful editor-in-chief of *Good Housekeeping*, thus becoming the only editor ever to edit *McCall's* and *Ladies' Home Journal* and *Good Housekeeping*. We remain friends today.

As for *American Home*, it failed the next year, giving me yet another reason not to regret my decision. I am realistic enough to know I could not have saved it; it would have failed regardless of what my efforts might have been.

Getting Down to Serious Management

After the announcements and the celebrations of my new exalted position, I had to figure out exactly what an editorial director is supposed to do. This was not top management, to be sure, but it was top editorial management, and now I wanted to prove to Burnett that I was up to the job. It was time to really come to grips with management and leadership as disciplines rather than as something I did while I was not being the creative director of a magazine.

What I did not know, of course, was that the whole notion of management was undergoing a great deal of ferment among the people who study and write about such things. I also did not know that part of Bob Burnett's mysterious "plans" included bringing Meredith into the forefront of contemporary management practices.

As it turned out, I was headed, wide-eyed and innocent, into the world of strategic planning, experimental organization systems, management by objective and its variants, job descriptions, performance appraisals, productivity analyses, and a lot of stuff I'd never heard of. I was kind of like Dorothy in the *Wizard of Oz* saying, "Toto, I don't think we're in journalism any more."

✤ Urban Flashback

Sitting somber in chauffeured cars,
surrounded by music and other people's stares,
wondering,
if I could go back to laughing summer days
in '37 Chevrolet flatbed trucks
on dust-choking gravel roads.

Nodding with concern in padded conference rooms,
breathing cigar smoke and unscented deodorants,
wondering,
who here could recognize me
as I chopped at the threatening grass
and loosened the red sand soil
around the desperate cotton.

Smiling through dim rooms and light talk,
sipping something chic and soda,
wondering,
which of these ladies would bring
a covered dish and a quart of tea
to set among the prayers and songs
on the dinner grounds in the pine grove.

Chapter Thirteen

Perks and Privileges

I had a recurring nightmare back in the mid-eighties. These were the years I was riding high as president of the magazine group, traveling every other week or so between Des Moines and New York, most of the time on one of the company's Lear 55 jets. I would arrive at Teterboro Airport in New Jersey and be met by a limousine and chauffered into Manhattan where I would check into the hotel suite reserved for me, complete with stereo, VCR, exercise machine, a full wardrobe and toiletries—everything I needed for the home away from home. I didn't even have to pack; just jump on the plane and go. What a life.

The route from Teterboro was usually through the Lincoln Tunnel and up the west side, then across to the hotel on East Forty-Eighth. Part of the route was through low-income neighborhoods, places where men with windshield wipers appeared at every stop light to wipe the windshield and hold out their hands for a tip or where ill-clothed people holding paper cups would tap on the window and ask for a handout.

The limousine driver would wave them away. "Just ignore those guys, sir," he'd say. It was difficult to do.

I recall during those days another trip, to Houston, Texas, where I had to make a speech, then rush to the airport. My hosts said they'd arrange a "car." It turned out to be a white limousine of extraordinary proportions, even by limousine standards. As I entered that music-filled place of mobile luxury, I noticed street workers who had paused and were staring at the car. My reaction was, "These are my people. These are what I come from."

And I found myself wanting to say something like, "Hey wait. It's not like you think. I'm not some overprivileged, silver-spoon-in-the-mouth jackass. I'm a working man. Like you." How ridiculous that would have sounded coming from the buttoned-down guy in the long, white limousine.

Back to the nightmare: I am in a limousine and we are stopped at a corner. Suddenly the back door opens and two guys in ski masks point a mean-looking automatic weapon of some sort and start pulling me out of the car. "Just shoot the rich asshole," one of them keeps shouting. And I start screaming and wake up.

What do you suppose it meant? Something about my own feelings that I did not deserve that luxury while others were struggling? Something about my residual class rage, turned inward? Or, given the headlines of the day, just natural and understandable fear expressing itself through the subconscious? Your analysis is as good as mine. All I know is that nightmare disturbed my sleep over and over again in those days.

But it never disturbed me enough to want to give up the Lear jets and the limousine rides. Like every other executive, I was able to justify these luxuries as saving me time and effort when my time and effort were best expended on behalf of the company and not on hassling my way through the commercial air travel mess. And in fact, I believe the stockholders were probably very well served by the planes and the limos.

I'm not sure how well they were served by other things.

Confessions of an Accidental Businessman

For instance, I was invited to a board meeting aboard a boat on the Nile, with first-class round trip tickets for my wife and me on the Concorde. I was a guest and had no part in the board meeting; my assignment was to enjoy the trip. An easy assignment.

I remember also another board gathering, a no-luxury-too-great meeting in New Orleans where, because of my experience there, I was selected as the company's host. "What's the budget?" I had asked. "Don't worry about it," I was told. "There's a lot riding on this meeting, and we want our partners to be happy."

For the opening night reception alone, I arranged for a piroque (a boat) filled with ice in which were embedded bottles of champagne and on which were sitting the finest raw oysters in the world. For entertainment, I hired one of New Orleans' most famous jazz bands. All this was only the introduction to three of the best days New Orleans could offer.

Part of me was astonished by the extravagance of the perks I enjoyed throughout my career, but down deep—though the fear of being judged provincial would never have allowed me to admit it—I just got a hell of a kick out of all that attention and all that fancy stuff. When, as kids, we lower working-class southerners talked about being "in the high cotton" or "up among the high rafter bats," this was a lot of what we were talking about.

In college, I had one pair of shoes, so I borrowed or rented dress shoes from other guys in the dorm when I had a chance to go to a dance. What a trip, from borrowed shoes to two full wardrobes in two different cities. "Hot shit!" my old friends would have said. "There are no flies on *this* boy!"

The Perks Creep in Almost Unnoticed

It's difficult to say when the perks begin. We tend to think of them as the elaborate privileges top executives enjoy, but in fact perks—depending on your definition—can be much simpler and more widespread and can start much sooner in the career cycle.

In the early days at Meredith, my perks were fairly modest: joining a senior manager for a dinner interview with a candidate for a job or a lunch on the expense account. Just having an expense account was a perk.

On my first trip for *Better Homes and Gardens*, I did a travel article in an area of Tennessee I knew fairly well. The research would not be demanding, and I would get to see some family and friends. All in all, the assignment seemed to me like an expenses-paid vacation.

Upon my return to the office, I dutifully filled out the expense sheet and turned it in, exquisitely careful in accounting for the money. The next day, the managing editor called me into his office. When I entered, he was holding my expense sheet. I was anxiously running the numbers through my head when he said, "I need to talk to you about this."

"It's exactly what I spent," I said, preparing to defend the entries.

"Maybe so," he said, "but it's not enough."

"Huh?"

"I want you to be honest, but surely you spent more than this, surely you're forgetting something?"

"No, I'm not," I said. "I kept notes every day."

"What about this blank space by the dinner entry?"

"I ate with friends."

"Well, let's put down something anyway."

While saying in one breath that he wanted me to be honest, he filled in several meals I had not paid for, explaining that the guys downstairs would begin to expect all the editors to travel this cheaply. So I got some money back I had not expected and did not deserve.

This was my first exposure to the padded expense book, which is not an official perk but one that seems borne of some understanding or sense of entitlement, and one that I subsequently learned was widely used in business. The rationale seemed to be, "They expect me to spend a certain amount on meals and cabs and such, so if I'm willing to have a McDonald's hamburger, why not make a little profit for my inconvenience at being away from home?" I fell into that rationalization myself in the early years, but stopped when I finally faced up to the essential dishonesty of it.

The high point of perks for the down-in-the-ranks editors and salespeople was to leave winter behind for a conference in some warm and sunny resort. (I refer to this as a perk because that's the way I thought of it at the time; later, I came to realize the serious business value of such meetings and came to consider them an investment in morale and productivity.)

I remember remarking to a senior company executive at my first conference that I never expected it to be in such a beautiful, luxurious place.

"Well," he said, using what I now recognize as his good corporate vocabulary, "we try to pick places that will set the right tone, a combination of professionalism and relaxation."

"But it seems so expensive," I exulted, almost breathless.

"We also want to demonstrate to our people that we're willing to invest in their training and growth."

At the time, I had thought I would never work for a company that would send me to those kinds of places. I had the same reaction when I was assigned to attend trade shows or to cover product introductions. I remember vividly those early days when the sense of privilege was palpable, when I would check into a convention hotel and marvel at the luxury, when I would walk the grounds and stop by the pool bar for a drink, when I would sit on my balcony or patio gazing at the golf course or the beach or whatever the particular rich view happened to be, when I would pack my toilet kit with the extra little soaps and shampoos and shoe shine sponges to show my first wife as I described how swell the place had been.

But by the mid-eighties, I began to feel that I had been

to one damned conference too many, stood around one cocktail reception too many, shook one hand too many, heard one whiz-bang motivational speaker too many. Yet I took a lot of pleasure in watching the younger people's reaction to *their* first big expensive perk.

Some Perks Are Well-Justified

In recent years, perks have taken something of a bum rap. I admit it took a long time for me to get my head straight about perks. At first I asked, "Do I deserve this?" But the greater question was "Does anyone deserve this?" The answer to both questions turns on another one: "What do I have to do to get those perks?"

As a fighter pilot, the perks came as opportunities to travel, to take cross-country "training flights" which, because I was stationed in France, meant weekends in London or Copenhagen or Madrid or Munich or smaller cities in between. I recall sitting at the Phoenix Hotel in Ålborg, Denmark, eating cold North Sea lobster with toast and butter, drinking Tuborg beer, finishing it off with Aquavit, then taking a cab to the Ambassadeur Club where my fellow pilots and I danced with Danish girls who worked at the Aquavit plant or the cigar factory. The tempering element of that occasional good fortune was the knowledge that, in exchange for it, I was expected to do one of the most dangerous jobs in the world. I did not feel over-rewarded.

In business, the expectation for an executive is as simple if not as immediately hazardous: to commit anything it takes—time, effort, neglect of home and family—in order to get the job done. Does anyone ever spell this out? Rarely. Do most companies expect this? Yes. I agree with the argument that corporate executives work very hard and virtually define their lives in a way that accommodates their work and not the other way around. And I did that myself for a long time.

Generally, I support the use of perks at any level in an

organization as a way to make people's lives less stressful, thus more productive. I support the ones that boost morale and help build community. In other words, I think perks can be useful management tools as long as they don't take on the character of "special privilege" for only a few.

Some Perks Are Just Executive Ego Stuff

Unfortunately, as they have become ever more elaborate for the top executives and as the public has become more aware of them, perks have created widespread resentment among employees and the public. Though all perks have some ego-boosting element built into them, I am very opposed to the ones that do nothing but boost ego. And I would like to see boards of directors, in their current zeal to cut costs, reexamine perks to ensure that they do something to move the business forward by accommodating the executives' time in a way that makes it productive for the company.

They could start with luxurious offices, which generally are a waste of money, as are such power-based symbols as executive lunchrooms and washrooms, assigned parking places, wardrobe allowances, and so on. Again, if it is judged that those things somehow serve to move the business forward, fine. But I suggest that all this often becomes just a hidden part of the compensation package.

And I had my share of those pointless perks. One was my country club membership. Ostensibly, the membership is to accommodate business entertaining, particularly golf. I won't bother to argue with that, but as a non-golfer, a country club membership made no sense to me, so I did not join a country club for years after the time I was eligible to do so. Finally, in the late eighties, I joined, mainly because there was a good aquatics program in which my young son, Ronald, who has autism, could participate. Not a business reason but a good reason nonetheless.

But the old poor-boy block worked on me. Though there

were no discriminatory policies at this club, I just could not bring myself to go there alone or to take a guest for over a year. I went only to the kids' swim meets. I wouldn't even memorize my membership number so I could charge drinks and food; I had to ask my little boy.

My wife, Sally, finally asked, "What is it about the club that makes you so uncomfortable?"

"I think it is that I identify more with the help than with the members," I said.

It's a wonder I didn't have nightmares about one of the lifeguards jumping in the pool and holding me under until I drowned.

Finally, one day at a swim meet, I saw all the other parents urging Ronald onward and applauding him as he got out of the pool, and I felt for the first time a sense of community among those upper middle-class young professionals not unlike the sense of community in a country church or a fighter squadron.

My resistance dissolved instantly, and I began to use the club regularly for business lunches and meetings, though I would never claim that the club membership ever did anything to move my business forward.

The perks are gone now. Whatever I enjoy—club memberships, trips, resort hotels—I pay for myself. I still travel to New York on business, fighting the old airline crush through O'Hare. My wife and I try the good restaurants and go to shows. Sometimes she and I think that my years as a corporate executive conditioned us to more of that stuff than we can afford. On the other hand, it is our choice and the costs are clear, not hidden.

On a rare day, however, watching airplanes at the airport with Ronald, we see one of the Meredith Lears taxi out, take off, and turn east toward New York. Sometimes we tune in the Meredith frequency on our little VHF radio and hear the pilots talking to the hangar. I hear those familiar voices

Confessions of an Accidental Businessman

and occasionally I feel the old urge to be there with them, heading for that landing in Teterboro and the limo ride into the Big Apple. But most of the time I think, "Better them than me."

One other thing: That old nightmare seems gone forever.

✌ Airport Scene

I know a traveler in a hurry,
always fidgeting in the rampway,
who wants to paint a red line
on the floor at every gate
and announce "No hugging or kissing
before you reach the red line"
so other people,
especially him,
won't be delayed by all that affection.

Chapter Fourteen

Experiments in Management

My promotion was greeted with a lot of enthusiasm from the company's magazine editors and designers. That made me feel good. The title—vice president and editorial director of the magazine division—had a great sound to it, and it made for an impressive business card. That made me feel good too. My first week on the job revealed that there was a lot more to it than I thought, that the structure of the creative group was redundant and inefficient, and that I was going to have to do a major reorganization. That did not make me feel good.

Sometime along in there, Bob Burnett sent me and a few other promising managers to an American Management Association seminar in Chicago. Much of the presentation had to do with the treatment of employees and with various organizational forms. It was an enormously enlightening experience for me, affirming much of what I believed—and had learned the hard way—about management.

It was the first time I had heard informed, educated, and

experienced businesspeople criticize the rigid bureaucracy that seemed to develop in most large companies. Though I'd had my own criticisms of structure and organization and policy, I simply didn't feel grounded enough in theory to make valid criticisms. Thus it was encouraging to be exposed to new ideas about organizational development. I also realized that Bob Burnett had a motive in sending our group to the seminar: He wanted us to be challenging the status quo. Nothing could suit me better.

Giving the Matrix System a Try

There probably were managers at Meredith who came to believe that my AMA experience created an organizational monster, for it was there that I first heard of the matrix organizational system and realized immediately that our creative group would be the perfect place to put it into practice.

At the time, there were two editorial and design groups working under the "Better Homes and Gardens" heading: *Better Homes* itself and special-interest publications. There were separate food departments, home furnishings departments, crafts departments, and so on. It was clear to me that, say, every food story appearing under the "Better Homes" name, whether in the magazine or in a special-interest publication, should be produced to a single standard of quality, and that standard should be determined by the *Better Homes and Gardens* food editor. I felt it obvious that there should be one food department, one furnishings department, one building department, and on down the line, producing all the material in those subject areas regardless of where the individual article was to be published. Yet there needed to be administrative, budget, planning, and schedule oversight for the separate publications.

Easy, I thought. Complex but easy. Have all subject-matter editors (food, furnishings, etc.) report to the top editor in that category for creative and quality control, then "work with" and "under the direction of" the publication editors on matters of production, budget, schedule. This would fix responsibility for creative editorial quality and for management of the people with the expert subject editors, and fix responsibility for administration, budget, and production (management of the material, in other words) with the administrative editors. It just made sense to me that the content quality of every page with the "Better Homes and Gardens" name on it should be the ultimate responsibility of the senior *Better Homes and Gardens* editors.

I met with the top editors in each group, explained the concept, and enlisted their support. The reorganization itself, with all the accompanying memos and organization charts, seemed to go well enough, but there turned out to be a great gap between theory and practice.

The administrative editors felt disempowered—little more than coordinators. The individual SIP department editors who formerly had run their own operations felt demoted, as if they were not trusted to make those quality decisions without oversight by a "super" departmental editor. And despite the explanations, people—depending on their personalities—were confused about reporting relationships.

Add to this the old bugaboo that "nothing like this has ever been done in an editorial group before."

One morning in the hallway on the way to my office, I spoke to one of my most competent and professional department heads. "How're you doing this morning, Bev?"

"Hassled and busy," she said. "In fact, I might resign if only I could figure out who I report to."

It was not as messy as it sounds, and it was not as messy as the people thought, but it did upset traditional notions of how organizations are supposed to be set up. And it brought to the surface a lot of misunderstandings, even hostility, between the editorial groups—problems that threatened to undermine the potential good of my changes.

Sometimes a Conference Away from the Office and Out of Town Is the Only Answer

If I were advising a company today about how to make such a substantial change in structure and reporting relationships, I would encourage patience and I would insist that much of the groundwork be done from the bottom up rather than from the top down. I would require that senior managers meet with groups of employees to explain the concept, to ask advice, to seek help, and to build consensus. I would want assurance that most of the employees understood the plan conceptually and were willing to support it *before* I made any big announcements. And I would develop a good training program to support the changes.

But I wasn't that smart then, and the notion of groups of people working cross-functionally without the old Christmas-tree organization chart was considered revolutionary if not anarchistic. I had to do something to overcome the problems, to build a sense of community for the larger group without disrupting further the sense of community of the individual groups.

A senior manager at Meredith once said of me, "Autry sometimes thinks he's only one good conference away from solving all his problems." That was an overstatement, but I did (and do) believe in the power of get-away conferences to resolve a lot of problems, as well as to celebrate good work.

So I asked for the budget to take the entire creative group away on a conference. This was unusual in itself; conferences were the normal domain of the sales and marketing people. But I got the okay. Ostensibly, the purpose was to celebrate our product growth and to stimulate our creative thinking, but the real purpose was to get everybody away from the everyday pressures so that they could get to know one another as people and perhaps overcome some of the suspicions and antagonisms resulting from the reorganization.

To help in that process, I put together a glorious program; we brought in some of the best thinkers and creative minds of the day. We had workshops, big parties, good dinners, golf and tennis tournaments—in other words, we did all the things the "business guys," ad salespeople mostly, did at their much-ballyhooed sales conferences. At one of the last sessions, called "Ask Autry," I sat on a stool and just answered questions, no holds barred, about any subject: the organization, structure, budgets, salaries. I promised there would be no retribution regardless of the question. The people took me at my word, and after the session I felt beaten around the head and shoulders, but somehow it was a good feeling.

I'm not sure what worked, but something did. I suspect it was a combination of the place, the atmosphere, the program, and the demonstration of a willingness to spend money for just this group alone. Whatever it was, most of the antagonisms and misunderstandings were greatly diminished when we returned to our offices, thus giving the matrix system a fair chance to work.

We had a conference, sometimes in combination with the ad salespeople, for several years afterwards.

By the time I was promoted again in 1976, this time to editor-in-chief of books as well as magazines, the organization was working so well—far better than the previous organization—that we could inculcate the book creative group into our matrix system, thus taking the final step in bringing all subject matter quality and content under a single standard.

A contemporary way of looking at all this would be to call these groups "cross-functional teams," which is all the rage these days.

How to Get Ahead without Becoming a Boss

But there was still another experiment I thought the group could use. We called it, "The dual ladders to success." I got the idea from the practices of certain chemical companies who came up with a system to recognize and reward their scientists without requiring them to be managers.

As we know, most promotions put people into management positions at one level or another, regardless of whether the people want to be managers or whether they are qualified to be managers. This has created a myriad of problems over the years, turning great salespeople into awful sales managers or great writers into mediocre managing editors, and so on.

The chemical companies I heard about had established parallel promotion tracks for their scientists without requiring any management functions. For instance, one could become a "senior company scientist" with responsibility only for continued good research, bossing no one.

I felt this would be a good system for a creative group and decided to begin it in the graphic design department. With support from the personnel department (it was not yet called human resources) and from my boss, we established a senior designer position that could move to an assistant art director/creative position or an assistant art director/management position, depending on which part of the ladder seemed most appropriate for that person. Those qualified and interested in becoming managers could be on that track; those who wanted to manage no one but be recognized and rewarded for excellent design could be on that track.

I was so proud of myself for pioneering a system that had the potential to change forever the notion that everyone must be a boss to be a success in business. In theory everyone in the design department loved it, but once again, I came face to face with the fact that I was managing a group of human beings with all the individuality and unpredictability that implies. And once again, I learned a valuable lesson: *There are a lot of people who don't believe they really have a promotion, regardless of title or pay, unless they get to boss someone.* A frequent complaint was, "He is supposed to be on the creative side of the ladder, but he acts like the boss when he criticizes my work."

Still, today in my consulting work, one of the most frequent issues I deal with has to do with people's attempts to establish their authority—usually by trying to impose it on someone else—or with management conflict over who has authority to do what. This was a constant issue with the dual ladders experiment and required more management time than I'd expected to give it. Finally it worked, but some things work better than others, and some things are more difficult than others.

The only way I ever figured out to predict the difficulty of introducing a new idea was to determine how many egos would be threatened by the change, with each additional threatened ego making the chances for failure exponentially greater.

"Why did you try all that stuff?" I have been asked. I used to answer that the old systems just didn't work for a creative group, but my real motivation may have had more to do with my general response to doing business as usual. There just had to be ways to make work itself better for me and everyone else and to avoid the pitfalls of the same old Christmas tree organizational structure and the same old criteria for getting ahead. I admit there were times, though, when I wondered if my early negative business experiences simply had made me suspicious of "regular" or "conventional" approaches to problems.

Plans Are Worthless; Planning Is Everything

More and more through the seventies my life became one of senior management, more involved with other senior managers in the company, more consumed by budget, planning, and operations than by creative direction. In fact, I was even beginning to lose my sense of identity as an editor.

Even so, the senior management people of the company still considered me an editor, and most of them still considered the creative group to be a bunch of unruly, undisciplined, unpredictable, unconventional people. Editors and designers, particularly designers, seemed to make some of the "corporate types" nervous. One senior manager used to refer to me as the "zoo keeper."

I knew these stereotypes were wrong; I also knew that editors and designers would always be limited in their potential to change disciplines and become other kinds of managers if those stereotypes prevailed. So I set about to prove to the corporate people that the "creative types" could be good businesspeople.

We were successful, I believe, simply by approaching budgeting and resource management in a very businesslike way, changing our style as much as anything. Also, we established some productivity analyses, by page and by cost, to prove the efficiency of the group in using resources. Within a couple of years, we had gone a long way toward gaining the respect of the officers of the company.

Somewhere early in that decade, the company, like so many companies, embraced "strategic planning." It was the business obsession of the day, but I was not as taken with it as I was with matrix organizations or dual ladders. The whole notion that somehow we could plan the future was alien to me. I had never planned my future, and I knew that if I had, it would not have worked out. I had not planned the circumstances of my younger life; I had not planned to go into magazine work; I had not planned to be divorced; I had not planned to be a vice president. I felt I had sort of ricocheted from one thing to another most of my life, planning some things in the short term and falling into others along the way. I felt the same way about my business career.

I remember telling my friend Adolph Auerbacher, one of the senior publishers at the time, "Look, it's like flying. You prepare yourself for the basic stuff of flying, then be ready to do what you have to do when the time comes. I always had the view that if you crashed one day, that was the day you probably would have fallen off the ladder getting out of the plane and broken your neck anyway."

Adolph was no fan of strategic planning either, but he had a different take on it. "Here's the way I see it. We are always shooting arrows every day. So we look to see where the arrows are going, then we run up in front of them and paint a bull's eye where they're going to hit. So let's not make a big deal about it."

He was right, of course. Better to sign on and play the game than to protest. So the creative group added this to the list of business disciplines that editors and designers mastered in order to prove themselves.

Bogging Down in Bureaucracy

I came to believe deeply in the disciplined thinking that strategic planning required, but I did not like the highly structured and ritualized process of it. Our senior people would say, "Plans are nothing; planning is everything." Sounded great, but after the planning process became institutionalized, the easiest way to get into hot water was to do something not in the plan. I shudder to remember how many good ideas and opportunities we let go by because they were "not in the plan." Clearly, this was not Bob Burnett's intent, but other managers began to use the plan as a convenient place to hide or to cover their asses.

And the resources we wasted—time, talent, money—just in going through the ritual were sometimes unbelievable. It's a good thing no one ever did a cost study of the process for the board of directors.

The senior corporate staff would set aside a few weeks for strategic plan reviews, giving every profit center manager in the company his turn in the barrel (and if you know that old joke, you get my drift). The managers would wait their turn outside the main conference room, then file in to face the music. The corporate people reminded me of nothing so much as those stern elders in the Rembrandt painting featured on the Dutch Masters cigar box. In fact, I used to call them The Dutch Masters.

The instructions we received each year for preparing the plan always gave us the same message: "Simplify, simplify, simplify." But after a year or so in the review process, the managers came to understand the unwritten instructions: "Be damned sure you don't leave anything out." The result was a run on binders and copying machines for about two months before the plans were due. And the plans themselves were something to behold: colossal.

And let me not forget the jockeying for position in the review process. Being invited to the plan reviews became a status symbol, both for the corporate reviewers and for the profit center managers and their staffs. What should have been a gathering of half a dozen people became assemblies of thirty or forty, most of whom had nothing to contribute and many of whom would rather not be there but would have felt left out if not asked.

This process became for me a metaphor for the kind of constipated processes that robbed (and still rob) large companies of their flexibility. Plus, it was just a gigantic pain in the neck.

I try now to keep this in mind as I lead companies in planning workshops.

The Time Comes to Leave All Your Technical Duties Behind—And Try to Become a Leader

All this stuff—strategic planning, organization, compensation and reward systems—had their fascinations for me as journalist/writer/ editor; after all, no one in my job had ever done these things before. Plus the editorial management group and I had succeeded in proving that editors and designers would accept and embrace the harder-edged responsibilities of business.

Confessions of an Accidental Businessman

But the move upward into management always involves the painful process of letting go of the very skills upon which we established our reputations in the first place. In my case, as my time became more devoted to the management and administrative areas, I spent less and less time writing and editing. The die was cast.

And the next step came soon enough. It was at another Burnett meeting, this one in Carefree, Arizona, at a little Mexican restaurant. Sitting outside in the spring desert sun, Burnett asked, "Are you willing to take on a job on the business side? I mean, are you willing to become a profit center manager and run a business for us?"

I told him I'd let him know, but of course I knew that I would not be able to say no to Burnett if that's what he wanted me to do. So, within a day, I said, "I'll give it a try, but I warn you, I do not fancy myself a businessman."

"You are one already," he said, "and you've proved it to me. You just don't realize it yet."

Within a few weeks, he called me to his office to say that he wanted to promote me to senior vice president and general manager of magazine publishing. This meant I would go from being top editor to being the top magazine businessperson, with all the publishers reporting to me. This also meant I'd probably have several unhappy publishers on my hands.

It was once more into the breach, but I loved the thought of it. I loved being one of the few editors in the magazine industry to become the business head. I loved the idea of bringing another management style to that side of the operation. And I loved that this assignment was surely a big test, and that if I passed it, even bigger management jobs might present themselves: At the very least, I could become a group president.

Bob did not have to sell me on the move. Even though I knew this was the end of any pretense that I was still in a "creative" job, this reality no longer bothered me as it once did. I had begun writing poetry and was working on a book, and I felt a job on the business side might make me feel even freer to pursue my own writing. All I would have to do is get on top of the job so I'd have the time.

I discovered that the higher you go in a corporation, the more likely it is that the job will expand to fit the amount of time you are willing to give it. And I was willing to give it a lot, so my first three books—over a nine-year period—were written at odd hours, on airplanes and in hotel rooms.

Strangely enough, it was in the writing of poetry which, in many ways, is a search for meaning, that I began to look more to my work as a source of meaning in itself. And I began to realize that I had yet another big step to take on the way from manager to leader, and that was a step from the external to the internal. This meant I not only had to let go of the basic skills that brought me into the business, but I also had to let go of the management and administrative skills as well.

Then finally, I would have to let go of one other thing: my ego.

Chapter Fifteen

Mistakes and Blunders

O ne thing about being a pilot: There's no ambiguity in mistakes. When you make one, something bad happens, and if you make a big mistake, you die and you may even take others with you. It usually does not require a long period of analysis and evaluation to decide whether there truly was a mistake. Screw up, die. Simple.

Business is far more complicated. By the air force logic, it would be screw up, lose your job. More often than not, however, the consequences may not be yours alone to bear. If you are high up enough in the company or clever enough or well-connected enough, it may go like this: You screw up, other people lose their jobs.

There are different kinds of mistakes, of course, and that presents some problems of definition. Here's how I think about it.

Strategic Miscalculations

Strategic miscalculations are mistakes made from boldness and innovation, from well-considered risks and well-thought-out consequences and alternatives. Who knows why such risks end in failure? The business world is filled with retro-visionaries who will look backward and analyze what went wrong, but there are damned few who can call it ahead of time. When good operators take these risks and make these mistakes, they provide fall-back positions in order to minimize the damage to the organization and to the people. In other words, they live by the rule of never risking a mistake they can make only once. Business cannot grow without some strategic miscalculations.

I made such a miscalculation as a result of a dream, some faulty assumptions, and the capriciousness of the economy. Having helped start *New Orleans Magazine*, I kept in touch with city magazines and their progress around the country. It became clear that the same special-interest factors driving national magazines could also drive city magazines. I was convinced that city magazines emphasizing such things as homes and gardens were part of the future of magazine publishing; and in fact, by the early eighties, there were several city home and garden magazines.

There were also two large and formidable regional magazines, *Sunset* and *Southern Living*, which were sharply increasing the competition for advertising dollars. My dream was that the Meredith Magazine Group could buy or start a series of city home and garden magazines, package them together for advertising purposes, then sell *Better Homes and Gardens* advertisers on the advantages of buying national advertising in *BH&G* and local advertising in our city magazines. The key strategy was to build a network of such publications in desirable markets.

So when the opportunity to buy into two city magazines—*Houston Home and Garden* and *Dallas-Fort Worth*

Home and Garden—presented itself, I was already inclined toward a city magazine strategy. In the Texas deal, Meredith would become partners with two other well-known and successful publishers, and after a certain period of time and presumed success in establishing other city magazines, we would be allowed to buy out the partners. Fairly standard deal.

The end of the story requires very little explanation. The Texas oil economy went into deep recession, the economies of Houston and Dallas-Fort Worth declined markedly, and advertising and circulation dollars began to dry up, causing the nice cash flow of our magazines to dry up as well. This postponed, if not simply cancelled, our plans to expand into other cities. The dream faded further into the future, and the operation became not a particularly difficult financial problem but a long-term management nuisance requiring more time and attention than it was likely to be worth. We decided to cut and run, taking our losses and abandoning our strategy.

I was sorry about the failure, but it was a calculated risk that could have had a good payoff; we were able to absorb the losses and go on about our business. Also it was not the kind of mistake that precluded taking other strategic risks.

Careless Miscalculations

Careless miscalculations are, as they sound, simply mistakes of carelessness; these are insidious simply because they slip up on you. You've seen that poster of an old biplane crashed into a tree with the pilot walking toward the camera, captioned, "Flying in itself is not inherently dangerous, but it is terribly unforgiving of carelessness." Business is somewhat different. Despite all the talk of change and risk, I do not believe that most businesses are inherently high-risk, in that daily slipups are not likely to cause the imminent destruction of the enterprise. But no business can for long survive a culture of carelessness or thoughtlessness, a culture in which managers do not train themselves to see the consequences of everything they are involved in every day: actions, decisions, relationships. In other words, carelessness and thoughtlessness build up over a period of time, and, by the time you may recognize them, there are no quick and easy corrections. You can't just roll the wings level, pull back on the control stick, and recover.

My worst long-term mistakes in this regard probably had to do with choosing the wrong people for certain jobs, then failing to recognize the problem until it had caused all kinds of mischief. I suffered from a widespread management malady: For a long time, I thought my personal impressions would suffice in determining who was right for what job. Complicating that deficiency was my compulsion to rush in and fill up all blank spots in a conversation, so that if I asked a job candidate a question and he or she paused in answering, I was, more often than not, inclined to answer the question myself, then kid myself that the candidate's nods and smiles signaled agreement. It took a long time for me to just shut up, suppress my own discomfort, and sit silently until an answer came. Thoughtless and careless: After firing a few of those people, creating great pain for both them and me, I learned that the best way to prevent firing someone was to hire the right person. Seems simple, but I think that I personally had so often perceived myself to be judged and found wanting as a young person—which may not even have been an accurate perception—that I felt some unreasonable impetus toward "helping." It was no help.

There is plenty of other "kid-yourself" carelessness. A common one is the thoughtless disregard for clear signals that a significant change is on the way. In my early years as general manager of magazine publishing, I was not quick enough to respond to news of lagging newsstand sales or to competitive pricing moves by other companies. And I spent a lot of time in denial about the troubles of one of our magazines, ignoring or discounting the monthly bad news. Indeed, that magazine had a brief period of glory—thanks not to me but to the superior efforts of its staff—but eventually it was sold to another company.

Blunders

Blunders are just that: pure, dumb, thoughtless, careless mistakes that are the direct result of doing something wrong you most certainly should have done right. There are no explanations and there are no excuses. Many times, these are the mistakes that cost you the job.

I believe I made only one very big one and another modest-sized one. In the eighties, I was approached by a broker who was representing a crafts publishing company on the West Coast. It seemed remarkably successful, and it struck me as a very good fit, as well as an opportunity for growth. I asked to see "the book."

Anyone who knows anything about business knows that "the book," which is assembled by the seller, will present the best possible picture of the company. I knew that, but my excitement got away from me anyway. I shared the book with our chief financial officer, who also got excited. We immediately saw ways to buy this company, continue to build it, then spin it off as a separate company. It had us widening our eyes in exuberance, winking, and jabbing one another with our elbows. What a deal, if only we could negotiate the right price.

The CFO and I journeyed to the West Coast, talked with the owners and their representative, and made an offer; they accepted it. The offer, as is any offer, was contingent upon due diligence. This is where we failed. The people I sent to do the due diligence were overworked at the time, somewhat stressed by the pressure, and intensely aware of the CFO's and my desire to purchase this company.

They checked the circulation figures, ensured that all orders were verified and legitimate and that bills were mailed.

What they did not ascertain is the degree to which those bills were being paid ("pay-up rate," we called it) or, as the case happened to be, were *not* being paid.

We found out about the low pay rate many months after we took possession of the company. Needless to say, the depressed return on equity of that enterprise was a drag on the rest of my operation. It was not bad enough to cause a financial disaster, but it was a very big drag that cost a lot of money.

Please understand that I do not fault my people who did the due diligence. I did not give them enough time and I did not assign enough people to the job. The CFO felt considerable embarrassment and chagrin, but it also was not his fault. He did not know anything about magazine publishing, having recently come from another company, and he trusted me, as group president, to know what the hell I was doing. I do not fault the sellers because they were not accomplished businesspeople, and I truly do not believe they were aware of the impending problem.

In short, *I* blew it. It was a large blunder, the worst of my career. Fortunately, it was not large enough for me to lose my job, although my income was negatively affected—as indeed it should have been.

The modest blunder was one of those slip-up-on-you, one-little-mistake-after-another-until-it's-too-late blunders. In that category, I made one dilly of a mistake.

The late eighties saw a lot of hype about multimedia initiatives. Publishers would get into broadcast; broadcasters would publish; everybody would get into video and CD-ROM (whatever that was at the time) and online. I was always looking for ways to present advertiser customers with "packages" of advertising opportunities; and in fact, we at Meredith Magazines were doing a very good job of packaging our magazines along with custom publications of all kinds. We were producing custom videos as well.

Along came a television producer/director with a great

Confessions of an Accidental Businessman

idea. He wanted to put together a major TV special consisting of a variety show featuring big stars and shot on location at a large outdoor sports stadium. The show would be presented as if it were the entertainment part of a big picnic sponsored by one of our magazines. We would actually have a picnic throughout the day with families attending, eating, playing games, and all that. Part of these activities would also be filmed, then interspersed in the final show with the big-time, show-business acts.

According to the producer, Meredith would not be required to put up any money, but just lend our name to the picnic, then we'd split the proceeds from syndication rights. Sounded fine if the producer could actually pull it off.

I expressed one major concern to the producer: "Look, I know the Midwest and I know picnics. What if it rains, as it is very likely to do? Shouldn't we do this indoors?"

"No problem," he said. "We'll have rain insurance, which will reimburse all the costs."

Before I knew it, the producer had signed some very big acts, arranged the stadium, and contracted the film crews. It was a little heady, being a magazine guy in the midst of all this showbiz stuff. But it was also nerve-racking because the TV guys seemed so seat-of-the-pants about everything.

I confess that I had been warned about working with "television people." I had been warned about broken promises, inept plans, and creative accounting.

My blunder was in not drawing the line, and I had several chances to draw the line. First, we were asked to guarantee some of the logistical arrangements.

"They don't know me," the producer said, "but they know your company. I'll pay for everything, but they want your name on the dotted line."

"Okay," I said. Blunder number one.

I won't detail all the other little blunders along the way, but the night before the event, the producer came to me needing a check to pay the performers. "They won't go on without the money in hand ahead of time, and I can't get a cashier's check by tomorrow," he said.

"What?" I shouted. "You mean we are within twenty-four hours of this thing and we won't have a show unless we come up with this money?"

"That's the way it's normally done," he explained.

"This is a hell of a time to find out the procedure," I said.

The final blunder was in writing the check to cover those performance fees. Even with all the promotion and publicity, even with all the arrangements, even with all my hopes for a great show with great promotion possibilities, I should have just said, "Sorry, this was not part of the deal. If you can't come up with the money, you better call a press conference."

But I said okay and came up with the money.

Guess what happened the next day?

It rained.

Guess what the rain insurance policy said?

Something to the effect that it must rain a certain amount *at the airport* by a certain time in order for the policy to pay. Unfortunately, the stadium where the show was to play was nowhere near the airport. It rained plenty at the stadium but not much at the airport. Small wet crowds. Small gate income. Production problems. Drying down the stage between acts so the dancers wouldn't slip and fall. And on and on and on.

Still, there was the hope that the show could go into syndication and earn back most of the money. I still have a tape of that show. Despite the great talent, the show stinks. It did not earn back the money.

And most important of all: it was embarrassing. I'll skip the part about the lawsuits.

This whole sorry episode was a lesson learned too late about paying attention to my own instincts and my own misgivings all along the way. Somehow, it was as if I just turned off my bullshit detector every time that TV producer showed up; then I would take another small fateful step toward Blunder City.

The Worst Mistake of All

So I have made my share of all of these kinds of mistakes, but I know this: The worst mistake of all is "The Do-Nothing Mistake." Although I do not try to justify my own mistakes, Lord only knows how many companies simply languish themselves to death, satisfied that they are doing the right thing right up until the time that it's too late (or almost so) to do the right thing.

The big mistake of doing nothing often occurs, I think, because companies in their smugness and in their concomitant fear of change become so institutionalized, with burdensome and awkward and repressive policies and procedures, that they simply cannot get a decision made. In my visits to and my working with companies in many industries, I hear the same complaint: "It's too hard to get a decision that lets us actually *do* something."

Jet-fighter pilots, longing for a more seat-of-the-pants, less technologically driven age, used to tell the story of the caveman who won fights by hitting his enemy with a club. One day, an enemy put a rock in his club, and the caveman ran. The next day, the caveman put a bigger rock in his club, and then the enemy ran. The next day, the enemy appeared with two clubs, swinging both. The caveman ran. The next day, the caveman took aim and threw his club, just missing the enemy as he ran. The next day, the enemy threw his club farther, and the caveman barely escaped. The next day, the caveman appeared with a sling on his club so that he could swing the club around his head and give it a high-velocity throw. The next day, the enemy showed up with a sling on his club. The two faced each other and began to swing their clubs. The only problem is that they took so long in winding up and building the velocity, a third caveman came out of the forest with a small club and killed both of them before they could get their clubs up to speed.

We do the same thing in business. We make our systems

and our procedures and our checks and balances so baroque and complicated that ideas get bogged down while our competition has all the chances in the world to slip up on us.

And we build cultures of fear in which managers put more effort into ensuring that they do not make mistakes than into doing something that might be productive. These same managers then write "C.Y.A." memos and things go on as usual.

C.Y.A.: "Cover Your Ass."

The worst mistake of all.

✑ Jeopardy

I.
How many times have I died?
At least once on the motorcycle,
with Jack Spencer on the back,
the unexpected cars
and the boy on the bicycle
and nothing to do but skid and hope.
Or run off the road
by the Cadillac passing on the hill
outside Holly Springs.
And certainly in the F-86
over the cotton fields below Rabat
with Dickie on the radio

Jesus, Cowboy, pull up before you roll!

(Think of that,
of all the hoeing and picking,
of all the sun hot hours in cotton fields,
to hang my wing
and tumble into bloody pieces
on some foreigner's cotton
ten thousand miles from my people's land.)

And in the fog at Wethersfield
in an Englishman's pasture
with sheeplike gray boulders
in a wash of green
only a hundred yards from the runway
but far enough that all I could say
was Oh Shit.

And in the whistling silence
of a dead engine.

And in a thunderstorm
that rolled back and wrinkled the metal skin
like old time cigarette paper.
And in a hundred things I didn't even know about.

II.
There are courts of inquiry somewhere,
accident investigators piecing it together.
There are coroners,
there are undertakers trying to make me
look okay after all.
There are caskets shipped back
filled with rubber sacks
not nearly full enough.
There are honor guards clicking their heels
and firing rifles in country cemeteries.
There are proud mothers
and wet-eyed widows
and children with pictures for fathers.

III.
But through all those deaths,
I am here,
still and again,
with at least one to go,
and the only thing changed
is the limb I am out on.

Chapter Sixteen

The Rocky Road
of President
in a Golden Age

My appointment to vice president and general manager of magazine publishing coincided with the beginning of the eighties. It was a decade where tastes were driven by the middle-class baby-boomers who turned out to be the most acquisitive generation in history, far outdoing their fifties parents. These new family people gave us everything from designer food to designer children and seemed preoccupied by neo-everything—from nouveau Beaujolais to neoclassical architecture. They bought stuff—God, how they bought stuff—and they wanted the stuff they bought to reflect status and affluence and quality, and they wanted it to look good. Above all, they wanted it to look good.

In other words, it was a perfect time to be in magazine publishing, and once we got past the recessionary years and into the mid-eighties, it turned into a golden age for magazines.

But the decade did not begin well for me personally. Once again, I faced divorce. This is a painful subject because I am embarrassed about my marital record—ashamed of it in fact—and cannot talk or write about it without wondering why it took so long for me to get things right.

I have no excuses for my two divorces and three marriages. I am now as happy as I can imagine being, but that does not lessen my sense of shame and failure, my regret at having divorced my older sons' mother as indeed my father divorced my mother.

I can't explain the second marriage and its subsequent end except to say that, by the late seventies, Dorothy was living in New York and I was living in Des Moines, and we were much more friends than spouses. Perhaps that was always the case.

My present wife, Sally, was a food editor in the creative group, later becoming senior food editor of *Better Homes and Gardens*. Her presence in my life seemed from the beginning like a great gift, certainly something I did not deserve. I was scared to death to get married again; however, Sally did not give up on me, and after a relationship of several years, we were married in 1982. Our son Ronald was born a year and a half later, beginning the greatest adventure in our lives and setting in motion events that would lead in eight years to my early retirement. But more about that later.

How Power Changes

In my first few days on the job, I received gracious welcoming notes from the publishers, all of whom now reported to me and were responsible to me for the financial performance of their magazines. I in turn was responsible for financial performance to the president of the publishing group, Jack Rehm, who—until these changes—had been my counterpart and equal colleague in the organization

The change I noticed most immediately about my new position was in the tenor of the meetings. Editorial meetings, even budget meetings, had often been raucous affairs with everyone participating regardless of position in the organization. As editor-in-chief, I might offer an idea only to have it

Confessions of an Accidental Businessman

pounced on and derided by some new graphic designer three months out of school. It was a healthy environment in which ideas had to stand the test of full discussion, focusing always on what was best for our readers. The group was not without conflict or bruised egos, but we always aimed for a standard that emphasized the work, not the personalities. The result was that my ideas were no more sacred in the creative process than anyone else's, although I had final approval and responsibility for what we published.

It was different on the business side. In one of my first meetings as general manager, I offered an idea. It was met with silence, then the people involved went off ostensibly to give it a try. I believe they would have saluted had we been in uniform.

A week or so later, they returned to tell me that my idea had not worked. "We tried it, Jim. Didn't work." It dawned on me that they knew from the beginning that it would not work. Why hadn't they told me, as indeed any junior editor or designer would have?

This was a lesson not only in power and how people can take it from you but also in the management ethic so prevalent in American business: You tell someone what to do, they go off and do it, or try to, or say they tried to.

I knew I was going to have to use another approach. Clearly, the business people were going to be more comfortable with a more autocratic style, something they were used to. But I had spent years coming to a management style that attempted to engage everyone in the decision-making process. I did not want to depend on fear or intimidation to get results because I felt—and still feel—the results would always be fleeting.

Numbers Tell Their Own Story, If You Know What to Look For

Yet in those days, I was having trouble just finding the vocabulary for communicating with some of the people. On the one hand, I felt that I had a lot of educating to do, and on the other, I felt that there was a lot of educating I needed before I could start educating anyone else.

Of course, I had dealt for years with budgets and budget planning involving the expenditures of many millions of dollars; but never before had I been responsible for revenues. One way of looking at the creative group was to classify it as just "one big cost center." Hell, I didn't even know how to read a balance sheet, and although I could read and understand an operating statement, I was learning that the numbers do not always mean what they seem. There are implications invisible to the untrained eye. Same with a balance sheet.

During those years, I developed a deep appreciation for the people I had thought of as "numbers crunchers." I discovered that there is a high level of creativity involved in financial analysis and that a good financial analyst relies as much on intuition and judgment as does a writer or designer. I'm not talking about finding loopholes or doing accounting tricks; I'm talking about the ability to look at a page of numbers and discern patterns that point to an action or plan or process that just is not visible to the average well-educated financial person; I'm talking about the ability to make more money for the company than five good salespeople combined. I was blessed with several of these good analysts, Dean Pieters and Max Runciman high among them.

The more familiar I became with financial matters, the more I understood both the reluctance of so many profit-center managers to make decisions and the courage involved in making decisions, because there is no such thing as one single decision.

I recall a science fiction story in which a man pays a time-travel company to send him back to the dinosaur age for a big-game hunt. Everything was carefully planned—where the creature would fall to earth, the extraction of the bullet, the path the hunter would walk back to the time machine—and the man was warned not to vary in any way from that path.

He entered the machine, went back in time, shot the dinosaur, extracted the bullet, and walked back to the machine, everything by the rules except one: He could not resist plucking an exotic butterfly from a flower. After he touched it the butterfly could no longer fly and fell to the ground, where he left it fluttering as he entered the machine. When he returned to the present, the people looked different, were speaking another language, and were not expecting a time machine to land in their midst. They killed the man.

Financial decisions are like that. Sometimes you have no idea what chain of events you'll unleash by making one little casual decision, and those events could well end up putting your job in jeopardy.

What a shock that was to an ex-editor whose decisions surely could have some critical impact on the magazine itself but could also, in ninety-nine percent of the circumstances, be corrected in fairly short order. I learned quickly to ask Dean or Max for a review before deciding anything financial.

It was another of those critical lessons: *Even with care, there still is no such thing as one single decision.* One always leads to another. No wonder it's so difficult to get a junior manager to stick his or her neck out.

So I spent a lot of time learning the vocabularies of finance, advertising sales, and direct marketing. Just as I had worked to establish the credibility of editors and designers as good businesspeople in the management of their operations, I needed to establish my own credibility in disciplines very new to me. I needed to recognize the pressure points in those areas. Without this knowledge, there would be no way to gain—or more important, to deserve—respect from the people of the business side, most of whom no doubt shared the opinion that people in the creative group were at best eccentric, or at worst insane. Either way the "creative types," as they were called, did not conform to how things are supposed to be done. The suspicion was that I, as former head of that group, must be carrying a lot of the same baggage.

Always Look for Mentors

Fortunately, I was able to find two mentors. I had worked with both men for several years, and now they reported to me; nonetheless, they were not reluctant to give advice and information about my new job. One of them was Wes Silk, publisher of *Better Homes and Gardens*. It turned out that Wes himself had recommended me for the general manager's job. The other man was Adolph Auerbacher, perhaps the smartest magazine business guy in America.

Adolph almost lived and breathed wise aphorisms. Once early on, when I was faced with the problem of a very unproductive department made up of people who had sort of been shuffled aside, I asked Adolph his advice. "The only thing worse than a person who quits and leaves," he said, "is a person who quits and stays."

Shutting down that department and arranging for the early retirement of the men involved was a turning point in my career, both my management career as well as my writing career.

The department had been set up as a department with purpose; but after some years, the changing marketplace undermined its purpose, so it then became a place to put people who were not performing as well as the company would have liked. As I contemplated shutting it down, I realized that department was symptomatic of a widespread malady in business: the fear or the unwillingness or the inability to be honest with people, to tell them when they are not performing. It was far easier to just create a job and give people the old "shuffle off to Buffalo" than to critique them honestly and help them become better performers. Out of sight, out of mind.

I believe the managers who did that convinced themselves that they were doing the right thing, the humane thing, the compassionate thing. Nothing could be less true. People are not fools; they realize when they are being given "make work" and do not really have a purpose. Even these men who had been fine salespeople in their day, and thus were able to sell themselves on the importance of their jobs, knew in their hearts that the department had become a shell of its former self.

So, as I found myself that morning in New York, preparing to meet with the four men and to tell them of their fate, I felt that I was inheriting a job that either should have been done before or should have been prevented by giving these guys another chance to perform, perhaps in another setting.

Understand that Meredith was a good company as far as the early retirement was concerned. The men would be okay financially, and their retirements would be celebrated with all the dignity and attention they deserved for their years with the company. But as I faced them that morning and told them what was happening, I realized in the after-silence of my comments that I was taking something very precious: a large part of their lives and a large part of who they were.

Although I had been writing poetry for several years and had published a book in 1983, I had never written a poem about business. On the way back to Des Moines that day, I took out a pad, intending to do some work, and wrote my first business poem, "On Firing a Salesman." I put it aside for a couple of years, then finally read it at a speech I was giving on management. After the reading, the crowd was silent; when I looked up people were looking at their hands or at the ceiling, and I could see tears shining in some of the men's eyes. Then the applause came. I discovered then that I was on to something very important.

✑ On Firing a Salesman

It is like a little murder.
taking his life,
his reason for getting on the train,
his lunches at fancy restaurants,
and his meetings in warm and sunny places
where they all gather,

these smiling men,
in sherbet slacks and blue blazers,
and talk about business
but never about prices,
never breaking that law
about the prices they charge.

But what about the prices they pay?
What about gray evenings in the bar car
and smoke-filled clothes and hair
and children already asleep
and wives who say
"You stink"
when they come to bed?
What about the promotions they don't get,
the good accounts they lose
to some kid
because somebody thinks their energy is gone?

What about those times they see in a mirror
or the corner of their eye
some guy at the club shake his head
when they walk through the locker room
the way they shook their heads years ago
at an old duffer
whose handicap had grown along with his age?

And what about this morning,
the summons,
the closed door,
somebody shaved and barbered and shined
fifteen years their junior
trying to put on a sad face
and saying he understands?

A murder with no funeral,

Confessions of an Accidental Businessman

nothing but those quick steps outside the door,
those set jaws,
those confident smiles,
that young disregard for even the thought
of a salesman's mortality.

Discovering the Universal Experiences of Leadership

I realized through facing those men in New York and through the response of that audience that there are universal experiences managers have, experiences that provoke deep emotional responses but never find a voice and are never expressed because there is no forum for that expression. In fact, there is not even a vocabulary for it. I vowed to help find that vocabulary for touching the emotions of what we do, of how we engage our work in the corporate world. And I vowed not only to write more about it but also to bring it into my everyday work. I vowed to be even more emotionally honest as a manager than I had been.

This has much to do with the transition from manager to leader being fundamentally a leap from the external to the internal, from the life outside to the inner life, from a preoccupation with doing to the acceptance of being as the defining characteristic of leadership.

I vowed also to be more accessible physically as well as emotionally. The farther I went up the corporate heirarchy, the less time there seemed to spend with the people whose work helped me get there in the first place. Between my company officer colleagues and top staff people and customer contacts and industry responsibilities, I was left with little opportunity to talk and listen to the people closest to what was going on. That had to change.

There was a lot of talk at that time about "management by walking about," which seemed a good idea to me. But I soon discovered it could backfire. It is one thing to be accessible; it is quite another to just pop in on people as they go about their work. It scares hell out of them. I had to be accessible in other ways: meetings, informal coffees, sitting with groups in the cafeteria, and so on. And I had to fulfill the two principal and fundamental requirements of leadership: pay attention and listen. I'm still not sure I achieved everything I had hoped.

Missing Out on the Top Job

In 1986, there was another of those fateful meetings with Bob Burnett, and it was a classic of misunderstanding.

I had heard a lot of talk about the "competition" between my colleague (and boss at the time) Jack Rehm and me to become Burnett's successor. Bob had made no secret of the fact that Jack and I were his "people," and he had given both of us substantial opportunity to show what we could do.

It truly had never crossed my mind that I might become president of the Meredith Corporation, but the rumors got my attention. I talked with my wife—we had been married only three years—about that kind of future, the all-encompassing corporate kind of future. We had a baby by then, and neither of us was sure we wanted the family pressure that job would create, regardless of compensation and perks. Nonetheless, I decided to express that ambiguity to Burnett, holding out at least the possibility that he should consider me.

I began the conversation by saying, "Bob, I'm really not sure I want to be president, but . . . "

"Too late," he interrupted. "It's already in the plan."

I'm sure I flushed because I had a hell of a hot flash. Of course I had meant president of the company, but that's not what he meant.

"I'm moving Jack, dividing the magazine and book groups, and making you president of the magazine group. The group is too large to be part of something else."

"What about Jack?" I asked.

"He's going to have a top job in corporate with all the corporate staff reporting to him."

"He won't be in operations?" I was incredulous.

"Not for the time being."

So, either the die was cast and the successor was chosen or this was another phase in the process. I didn't make that point, however, and I made no attempt to "think over" the group president's job. I knew I wanted it. I knew the time was right to be starting new magazines and expanding Meredith's presence as a major magazine publisher.

I had not been in the job long, however, before a major event demonstrated to me that the top spot was to be Jack's, though I still was not even sure I wanted the job.

The event was the acquisition of *Ladies' Home Journal* for ninety-two million dollars, the largest acquisition in the company's history. I was excited. Just think how it would be to suddenly be publisher of two of the largest magazines in the country. A quantum leap in everything, from revenues to influence.

But then it happened. Burnett told me that the *Journal* was not to be part of my group; it was to be assigned to Jack, for his oversight and guidance in its integration into the company.

"Bob," I pleaded, "you wouldn't buy a television station and not put it directly in the broadcast group. Why this?"

"You already have a lot on your plate," he said. "Besides, this is temporary. After a transition period, it will become yours."

I'm not sure how anyone else in the company read this move, but it was a sure, clear signal to me that Jack was to be the next president of Meredith.

Though I had never really considered myself a competitor for the job, I confess I was disappointed that the possibility had passed. At the same time, Sally and I were relieved.

And I was happy for Jack. I had worked with him for years and most recently had worked directly for him. Our styles were considerably different, and I did not much like working for him. He was not mean-spirited, however. To the contrary, he was fair, he was honest, and he was always above-board. To say I did not much like working for him is not to say that I did not like or admire him personally. He lived his personal life to a high ethical standard and he did the same in his business life.

And as a minor stockholder, I certainly cannot complain about how the stock has performed during his tenure.

Depend on the People for the Big Payoffs

After the *Journal* episode, I plunged into what turned out to be several years of furious activity developing new magazines. In the years between 1980 and when I took early retirement in 1991, the magazine group went from four magazines to seventeen, including the *Journal* acquisition. It was even more than that if I counted the newsstand-only special-interest publications that became quarterlies.

Except for the acquisitions, all those magazines were developed through volunteer work. We did not hire a big R&D department, as did so many other publishers, some of whom launched the most expensive magazine blunders of the century.

I simply gave editors and designers the opportunity to volunteer to work on developing new magazines *on their own time.* The process was simple: "If you want to do it, sign up. We'll put together a working group or committee or task force."

We were overwhelmed with interest, so I took the entire group to one of my favorite places, Callaway Gardens, Georgia, for a three-day brainstorming conference. There were so many ideas, we had to set some priorities and then let people who "championed" those magazines serve on the team to develop them. Their only reward would be possibly to serve on the staff of the new magazine if and when it went through all the testing and was launched.

In those several years, we started many new magazines.

We produced and marketed some award-winning videos. We explored other media possibilities, though not profitably. I believe it was the most creative, the most vibrant, the most energetic, and the most productive period in the history of the company. My friend, employee, and mentor, Adolph Auerbacher, became one of the cornerstones of this development, and I began to call him the "Father of New Magazines." Damn, we had fun.

Just in the midst of all this new product activity, however, the economy began to start downward, and advertising sales became extraordinarily competitive, as did newsstand pricing. Also, one of our magazines that briefly had been profitable began to go downhill again. It might not have been so bad had I not made a couple of the costly mistakes detailed in Chapter Fifteen.

There were smaller misjudgments as well but all, I believe, in the category of acceptable risk given the imperative we felt to be trying new media, new promotions, new ideas of all kinds.

These glitches probably not only damaged my credibility but, more important, it hurt our earnings. We never were in danger of losing money—in fact, the group never stopped being the heart of the company's revenue and profits—but our margins began to slip sharply.

Here's where the hard choices hit me: Abandon the new product development and put that money back into the profits or ride out the economic problems with the confidence that when the new magazines became profitable and no longer required extra resources, they would return the margins to their previous levels. My own income was also a factor in the decision, as it would have increased substantially if I had put the money back into short-term profits.

I stuck with the product development, though I knew some of it was money down the drain. Don't call it courage; it was common sense and perhaps an uncommon optimism about magazines generally and our magazines specifically.

Refusing to Be a Pawn in the LBO Game

All this entrepreneurial activity within a large corporation did not go unnoticed in the business world. Remember, the eighties were a time in which business replaced sex as the most talked-about subject among the baby-boomers. I even tried to talk my son into giving his rock and roll band a business name, such as "The Corporate Staff" or "The Downside Contigencies."

Deals and LBOs were all the rage, and to be noticed in business meant really being noticed. Fundamentally, I felt this kind of attitude about business brought a gamesmanship that was not in the best interest of anybody's business. There was far too much emphasis on companies or divisions of companies as commodities that could be bought and sold and far too little emphasis on the productive doing of business. Concomitant with that was a dehumanizing of companies, an undermining of their community aspects.

But we were all susceptible to some degree. We talked a lot about the deals, watched the *Wall Street Journal* and the newsletters, and I knew several people who had become wealthy through LBOs. After I had been president of the magazine group for a couple of years and in the midst of all our new magazine start-ups, I received a call one day from an investment banker with one of the largest firms in New York. This man said he specialized in publishing properties and asked that I meet with him and some of his colleagues to discuss the possible leveraged buyout of the magazine group from the Meredith Corporation.

I declined. "Besides," I said, "you're talking to the wrong guy. I don't have the power or influence to make such a thing happen even if I wanted to."

He persisted. "It won't hurt anything to talk," he said, "and you might discover that the right amount of money can give you the chance to make something happen. Plus it could be an opportunity for everyone to do well, the company and

Confessions of an Accidental Businessman

you." I was intrigued, not so much with the potential for a "deal" as with the process and the experience of meeting with a group of these famous money guys. I knew there were were two strikes against any such deal: (1) I would never participate in it; and (2) It was not possible to do without the Meredith board's agreeing to break up the company.

I went down to the fabled Wall Street area to the right address and was escorted to a conference room with a spectacular view. I felt I was in a movie.

There were five men around a gigantic conference table. After we were introduced and had coffee, the apparent boss walked in, a little late, griping about the "damned Jaguar" that had given him trouble. He was about the age of my older son, slim, a smoker with a cordial manner.

The man who had called me laid out his plan. It was typical and simple. We would buy out the magazine group from the parent company, using debt that we could service with the group's considerable cash flow, a figure I did *not* reveal as indeed I did not reveal any confidential information. Still, they knew a lot. Then we would build up the earnings and sell to a larger company within a few years.

There was one short, heavy, baby-faced man who spoke with that kind of smirking arrogance that, in my elementary school, would have branded him a "know-it-all," a name that in high school would have given way to "smart-ass." If I had been even slightly tempted to cooperate, he would have blown the deal.

He said, "I know there is a lot of fat in that operation, and we could squeeze out another three, four million dollars in cost savings."

"Have you forgotten that you are talking to the person who now runs that operation?" I asked. "If there were a discretionary three or four million dollars available, don't you think I'd put them on the bottom line now?"

"Not necessarily," he said. "I can always find money the present operators can't find."

I must have turned red because I was pissed. What I wanted to say, reverting to my southern-boy rhetoric, was, "Listen, you piggyfat asshole, what do you know about managing a magazine operation? You clearly can't manage to even fit your ass into your suit pants."

But what I said was, "I guess it depends on your definition of fat or discretionary. I wouldn't be willing to cut back on new product development, which would hold the future hostage to short-term profits. In short, I think you have a fairly narrow view of magazine operations, Mr. _____."

Then I said, "As I said at the beginning, you are talking to the wrong guy. You should contact Jack Rehm if you want to pursue a deal. I'm not the appropriate person for a couple of reasons. One, I'm just the wrong guy organizationally, and two, I think what you people do is destroying American business, loading it down with debt, causing layoffs and cuts in quality. All this is about a few people making a lot of money, and it would violate my own ethical standards to do it."

"Then why have you wasted our time?" the young boss asked.

"Fair question," I replied. "I guess I wanted to see if what I've been reading and seeing in the movies is real. I've wasted both our time. I apologize."

But I'll give them credit for persistence. As I started out the door, Mr. Piggyfat shook my hand and said, "I appreciate what you've said. But think about it." Then he handed me his card.

The Most Difficult Decision of All: Giving It Up

Somehow between 1986 and 1991, everything came together for me professionally. I felt I was at the apex of a career in publishing: I was still learning and growing and developing. I was proud of what I was doing. And even though I could have made decisions that would have produced more personal income for me, I still was making a very handsome income, more money than I ever dreamed I could be paid. It seemed a long long way from the woods of Mississippi and the streets of Memphis.

But there was a rub: I was not home enough. It would be too simple to say that my first marriage failed because of my career, that my second marriage failed because it was more about careers than about marriage, or that I gave up my career finally because I needed to be with my third wife and our young son. Nothing about marriage can ever yield to such glib and pop-psychological explanations, yet there is truth in that summary.

When Ronald was an infant, he did not meet the milestones parents and doctors watch so carefully—such things as rolling over, sitting up, crawling, talking, and so on. He simply lagged behind on everything, far behind in some cases. We did not know what was wrong, only that something was. After a year, Sally resigned from her job to stay home.

One afternoon, the pediatrician came by our house and, with tears in his eyes, said, "I've been hoping Ronald was just developing slowly but we'd better run some tests."

There were a lot of tests, in Des Moines and New York. After Sally and I were told finally that Ronald had autism, it was clear that his needs and our desire to be together would bring about some major change. Five years later, in 1990, we decided that if it were possible for me to take early retirement and still have enough income for us to live and to provide for Ronald's long-term future, I would do it.

In the fall of 1990, I wrote two "white papers to myself," then shared them with Jack Rehm. As soon as I decided to let Jack see these writings, I knew I had decided to take early retirement, at age fifty-eight, with seven years in a good job still to go and perhaps as much as six million dollars in income and stock options and such still to earn. It was a lot to leave.

But as a friend told me, and as I reported in *Life & Work*, I was "leaving the obviously good for the somehow strangely better."

And it has turned out that way.

❧ Leaving It All Behind

There were days when we still didn't get it,
that this wasn't like school or the military,
that we wouldn't graduate or get out
and leave it all behind.

We pitied the older guys
playing out their big-time businessman roles
as if most of them were not just some kind
of free-market bureaucrats.
Somehow we knew we'd do better
and we knew we'd be different,
without that need to cover our asses,
without that fear of failure.
We would give young guys like us
plenty of room to make us look good,
and we would ignore stupid policies and politics
and get rid of deadwood vice presidents
who wasted time and money and office space.
We would have the guts to take our money and run
before the job pushed us too hard
and the next title became too important,
before we found ourselves on airplanes every week
and in the office every weekend,
before our kids stopped caring if we were around,
and our wives drank too much
at too many ladies' luncheons
where they were going to have just a sherry
or one glass of wine,
before we got tired of smiling at every jerk
who might spend a dime with us,
before we ate every oversauced meal
and sniffed every cork and drank every bottle of wine,
before we went to every sunny resort
and heard every self-improvement speaker

and danced at every black-tie dinner
and applauded every chairman and program committee
and carried home every printed tote bag
and T-shirt,
and put every smiling group picture in a scrapbook.

Before all that,
we would get out.

Chapter Seventeen

Gifts and Offerings

The business world is full of gifts, or maybe the correct word is "presents." If so, the business world is also full of gifts but they are not the kinds we usually think of.

During the holiday season, I received presents from photographers, production houses, printers, public relations firms, writers, contributing editors, paper companies, and miscellaneous vendors. In my early years in business, I thought of these as a bonanza, another perk.

The most elegant of these a junior editor could receive was from the Hedrich-Blessing studios in Chicago. The "Hedrichs," as they were called, were the best architectural and interior photographers in America. Not only that, they were splendid people to do business with. They certainly were not obliged to get our attention with gifts; they were obliged to nothing but their best work. Still, every year's Christmas present was a major project. They always wrote and printed a story about the quest for this year's gift and included the story in a special booklet accompanying the package. Inevitably it was something exotic found on one of their photography trips to some relatively unexplored place.

The sure sign that an editor had "arrived" at Meredith was to be included on the Hedrich's list. All the spouses of the junior editors checked with one another every year, fearful that they might have been left off the list.

But in fact, that gift was only a present. The real gift we received from Bill Hedrich, Jack Hedrich, Jimmy Hedrich, and their associate, G. Suter, was in all the training they gave us junior editors. After a photography session with the Hedrichs, in which the editor was supposed to be something akin to a director, the editor—if she or he was paying attention—returned with an education in photo supervision.

The Hedrich present, along with a dozen doo-dads of one sort or another from PR people, would show up in the weeks before Christmas. I would dutifully take them home, unopened, where my first wife and I would put them under the tree, to become part of our Christmas morning ceremony. Although the Hedrich presents were unique, it did not take many years for me to never want to see another paperweight or monogrammed money clip or pen and pencil set or ornament or calendar or graphic print or clever executive toy. During the holiday season, I was even happier that I was not a golfer and did not have to receive the office golf games or sets of balls or tees or one of those corny cartoons framed for display on my office wall.

Most of this stuff is a waste of money; virtually nothing of business importance occurs or results from all this present giving, and occasionally it gets out of hand and causes real ethical dilemmas. At one point, I banned a vendor's more outlandish presents which, by their very extravagance, was causing some of our people to feel obligated to do business with that vendor.

Recognizing the Real Gifts

Just as those kinds of material presents, even the great Hedrich presents, are inconsequential in the scheme of things, there are others I will never forget. These are the important ones, the ones that might more properly be called offerings. Several come to mind.

As I approached early retirement, there was an outpouring of affection and good will that, at times, almost overwhelmed me. In fact, I was so often moved to the edge of tears that I feared I was becoming what my grandmother used to call a blubbering old fool.

The New York advertising staff of *Better Homes and Gardens* hosted a lunch for me on my last official trip there. At the end of the lunch, the advertising director gave me a copy of my own book, *Love & Profit*, with a special message engraved in it. Then he stepped aside and two guys came forward carrying a full-sized door with a ribbon and messages stuck on it.

It was a duplicate of the door to my suite at the Middletowne Hotel, number 512. It even had the emergency escape placard on the inside of it warning not to use the elevators in case of fire and with a red arrow marked "You are here." On the outside were cards and messages from the staff at the hotel, wishing me well. Since I had gone in and out of that door so many times, they said, they thought I should just take the door back to Des Moines. Can you imagine such a treasure from a group of New York hotel staff?

I go through that door every day, to and from my attic office where, at this moment, I am writing these words.

In the week before the official event, the creative staff threw a special retirement party in the photography studio, the cavernous subbasement of the building where the presses had been forty years earlier and which had been coverted to a studio. I had seen a thousand photographs—gardens, interiors, remodelings, crafts, Holiday decorations, fashion, food—set up and shot in that space, and now I was the subject of the day. After refreshments and greetings, I was escorted to a chair in front of a special stage that had been built for the occasion.

A play began. The scene was a courtroom in which my fate was to be decided: Was I to go to Heaven or to Hell? The prosecution said, "Hell," and my defense said, "Heaven." The lawyers were dressed in robes and were wearing English barrister wigs.

With considerable encouragement and applause from the audience, the prosecutor detailed all my business mistakes—bum acquisitions, failed magazines, unsuccessful and costly promotions, and yes, the picnic/TV show fiasco—and the defense tried to counter with my successes.

Corny? Yes indeed, corny, slapstick, and silly. But what an offering. And I don't even remember the verdict.

The Perfect Offering

My retirement was official on December 31, 1991. On December 23rd of that year, I received a call from Denny Goerndt, chief pilot at Meredith.

"I thought I'd take one of the Lears out for a check flight tomorrow morning. Would you like to go?"

I knew this was code for, "I'm going to let you do what you've always wanted to do and fly the Lear." But that's not what he said.

"You bet," I said, even though it was Christmas Eve.

"Bring anyone you want," he said.

The next morning, my brother-in-law, his two sons, my son Ronald, and I were at the hangar. We got into the plane. Everyone strapped in, then Denny said, "Here's your seat" and pointed to the command pilot's seat.

"The left-hand seat?" I asked.

"You're the pilot," he said.

A dream come true. I had sat in the back of the Lear so

Confessions of an Accidental Businessman

many times watching the pilots that I just knew I could fly that baby. I even had those fantasies of the pilots falling ill and my having to take over and land the plane. Right out of the movies.

Now was the chance to prove it. Of course, Denny managed all the systems, the technical things that have now become the most challenging part of flying, but I handled the controls. Took it off, maneuvered, then made two landings. And they were not half bad.

My brother-in-law had the video camera, so I have the whole thing on tape. After taking a few snapshots of the group, of me with Denny, and of the plane, we made our way home for what I confess was a rather anticlimactic Christmas Eve.

Understand that all this was perfectly legal. I am a licensed commercial pilot; Denny is an instructor pilot; and I'm sure he received some official approval to take me up. But still, to give up part of his Christmas Eve just to indulge an old jet-fighter pilot a going-away present like that was more than a present, more than a gift. It was an offering that I will never forget.

There were many others, small and large. As the retirement got closer, I received clippings and poems and letters. I received some of my own writings done in calligraphy.

At the retirement reception in the cafeteria, an event that I have always considered as close to one's own funeral as a living person should ever have to get, hundreds of people came through the receiving line. Many were in tears, a gift in itself. Others had photographs and mementos.

After the receiving line and a few comments by Bob Burnett and Jack Rehm, a cord was pulled, and a large paper scrim fell away to reveal a huge quilt comprised of squares made by people and departments all over the company. Each square had a personal message with particular meaning, some of them relating to incidents and episodes from years past.

Still, with Lear rides and mementos and quilts, the

greatest gifts came as these people, this community of work, spoke and recalled good times and bad we had experienced over the years.

And with these was another gift: I knew that I had tried management styles and techniques and theories and philosophies that were considered out of the mainstream. I had been criticized from time to time for being "too soft," for "letting people take advantage" of me, for "tolerating too many special arrangements" for people. At times, I found myself doubting that I was doing the right thing. For what I was attempting, there were no guidelines, few role models, and no case histories. I had to rely on instinct and intuition.

What the people in the magazine group accomplished was in itself the greatest gift. And the outpouring of support and affection at my retirement was the offering of affirmation. Who could ask more?

I think of this every single day as I enter the door marked 512 and go up the stairs to this very word processor.

And I am grateful.

❧ On Paying Attention

There came a time in my volunteer life
when I began to give in
to the seductions of righteousness
and to think of my work as a sacrifice
for the good of others.
I would make schedules no one should try
so that people would ask
how it was possible for one man to do so much.
It was a time of three speeches
and three cities
in one day,
and in all the scurrying
I did not want the delay
of a restroom conversation
with a hesitant little man
in a cheap new suit.
I needed a quick pee, five minutes to think,
and two minutes to get to the podium
But there he was,
with the side effects I knew so well,
the puffy cheeks, the swollen gums
as he smiled and told me he had a job now
and hadn't had a seizure in six months.
I gave him the quick back pat
and the smile,
never expecting to see him again.
But he sat in the front row
and smiled a greeting when I rose to speak,
the dignitary from the national office,
bringing word from Washington,
the National Commission,
the Hill, the White House.
He smiled too often
and over-nodded and made too much of his notes,

clicking his pen and turning pages,
back and forth,
as if studying what he'd written.
When our eyes met he smiled and nodded,
another guy, I thought, who wants people
to think he knows the speaker.
So I avoided looking at him
until he shuffled, crossed his legs,
and stretched them in front of him.

When I saw the soles of his shoes,
slightly soiled, less than a day worn,
I realized he had bought the suit and shoes
just for this meeting,
just to a hear a speech squeezed
into an afternoon between two cities.
He had looked forward to it,
planned for it,
put new job money into it,
and would make notes
so that he could remember always
what the important man came to teach.

But the lesson was mine to learn—
about sacrifice
and counting blessings,
about patience
and paying attention to teachers
wherever I find them.

Chapter Eighteen

Rules to Live (and Lead) By

Ihave just returned from Australia where, as a consultant, I spent a week with the employees of Murdoch Magazines and its owner and managing mirector, Matt Handbury. It was my fourth time there in the past three years.

Matt bought Murdoch Magazines from his internationally famous media magnate uncle, Rupert Murdoch. Strange term, *media magnate*, but I guess it's more efficient for newspaper reporters and commentators than "wealthy guy who owns a lot of media around the world."

I do not know Rupert Murdoch except by reputation, and his reputation varies depending on the source of one's information. But I have come to know Matt Handbury during the four years I have consulted for his company, and I consider him a friend. If Mr. Murdoch's reputation is close to an accurate characterization of the man, then Matt is a wholly different kind of person. I do not know anyone in business anywhere who tries so hard to do the right thing for his customers, for the community, for his employees, and for himself. He does not succeed entirely, but there is a greater sense of openness and connection in his company than in any place I have seen.

There was a time he was succeeding so well that I thought he did not need my services anymore. Consulting has some parallels with psychotherapy in that I feel an ethical responsibility to tell the client when my services are no longer needed, when the company is ready to move on without me. When I tried to tell Matt in 1993 he did not need me anymore, he disagreed, and as it turned out, his was the better judgment.

After my most recent trip, I felt as I had after the trip last year: that this was the most courageously honest group of people I'd ever met in business. There were times that all of us, working together in intense all-day sessions, were so emotionally spent we needed to resort to silence, one of our most effective tools.

"Matt," I said, at the end of the week as he was letting me off at the Sydney airport, "I feel profoundly grateful that you have given me this opportunity to be an instrument of transformation in your company." We both were tearing up.

"But," I added, "this does not mean I'm not going to bill you."

What I admire most about the culture of honesty at Murdoch is that Matt himself takes the lead. He is almost radically honest, trying always to be sensitive if not always tactful. He is honest with his employees, of course, but it starts with himself. Many times have I heard him say, after having been soundly criticized for something he'd said or done, "Well, at the end of the day, I can learn from that one." So many business executives are in denial about their own shortcomings that it is utterly refreshing to come across a man who is willing to confront his own shortcomings and to have his employees participate honestly in that confrontation.

The commitment to act beyond ego—to recognize when we are in denial, to retain humility, to correct our mistakes, and to learn from others regardless of their so-called status—

*is the commitment to grow personally and spiritually through
the work we have chosen to do.*

It took a long time for me to make that commitment,
but it came full-blown in 1981. When I made it, I wanted it
for everyone, particularly for my colleagues and employees.
Finding the vocabulary to communicate not only my commitment to my own growth but to their growth as well was
very difficult. I came closer to that vocabulary through poetry
than any other way, but of course the very form of it put off
a lot of people even as it was touching others.

Perhaps the most frustrating realization for me came
almost at the end of my corporate executive career. *Love and
Profit* had just been published, and I was becoming in demand
as a speaker and workshop leader. I was being quoted, my
work was being anthologized, but somehow I felt I was not
able to make much impact on my senior corporate officer colleagues at Meredith—with the obvious exception of Bob Burnett, who encouraged my speaking and writing from the
beginning.

Had I been able to tell my mother about this witnessing
and about my closest colleagues being less receptive than people all over the country, she probably would have reminded
me of the scripture about the inability to be a prophet in your
own land.

But I have never thought of myself as a prophet. My
story is fairly simple and it does not change. I believe the
world is full of hard-working people who are smart and good.
Some want to succeed in business; some don't. Was I smart
and good? Yes. Did I want to succeed in business? Yes. Did
I work hard for it? Yes. But that was not reason enough for
me to be a corporate executive with all the ensuing accoutrements. There was also the matter of chance. I often have
paraphrased the management book, *Ecclesiastes,* that the big
jobs are not always to the smart, nor high salaries always to
the hard-working, but time and chance happeneth to them
all.

What Leadership Is All About

So, forget measuring success by the standards of so-called status and income and measure it by how you feel about what you do. What do we deserve from our work? Simple: dignity, nobility, meaning, purpose. Whether we are the CEO or the mail room clerk, we *deserve* that from our work, and it is up to our leaders to provide us the opportunities for personal and spiritual growth so that we may find dignity, nobility, meaning, and purpose in our work. Providing those opportunities is what leadership is all about. How is it done? Who knows for sure? Read whatever books you find helpful, try whatever techniques feel right, but understand that none of it works without honesty, trust, courage, and self-awareness. I guarantee that you will not be able to provide opportunities for growth and meaning if you yourself cannot find meaning in your work. Most executives I know put in a lot of hours, but working hard is not enough. *Remember that burnout is not a crisis of time so much as it is a crisis of the spirit.*

What has interested and impressed me so much over the years is not the inhumanity of business managers but the humanity of them. The paradox is that it so often requires an extraordinary situation for the humanity to blossom. It is as if something unusual is required for us to manifest our humanity in the workplace, as if it is not allowed otherwise.

I recall one man being stricken ill, even after leaving the company, and Ted Meredith and Bob Burnett making a special arrangement for a care facility. Once when one of our editor's houses was literally being pushed down a hill by a landslide, Jim Riggs gave the staff a day off, rented shovels and a conveyor belt, then joined us for an exhausting day of shoveling and fighting that hillside. More than once was a Lear jet authorized for a specal humanitarian mission for one of the employees. And the accommodations worked out for the seriously ill are too numerous to mention.

Confessions of an Accidental Businessman

Why, I have always wondered, could this humane accommodation of individual human needs not become the dominant culture of a company, practiced every day in small ways as well as large? Why wait for a crisis?

Once again, it requires a letting go of old notions, of old attitudes, of old needs for the illusion of power and control. Once again, it requires acting beyond ego. So often in business, *the ego gets supported by knowledge and information, then wisdom becomes lost. So does common sense.* And wisdom and common sense are the difference between managing and leading.

The Main Things I Know About Leadership

If, from my continuing successful career, there are observations to offer about leadership, these are the main ones:

- **All growth and most good things come from paying attention.** Leadership is largely a matter of paying attention. So is life, for that matter. This means paying attention, and attending, to the relationships in our lives, whether with a spouse or child or friend or colleague or vendor or customer.

- **Next, use every experience.** Every experience is connected to every other experience, from childhood throughout our lives. Everything counts. Everything—every event, every episode, every interaction—means something. Look for that meaning and remember the most important things are not obvious to the eye.

- **Never think of employees as "labor," as a commodity.** Once we begin to think of workers as a commodity, we rob work of its meaning and we rob our people of their opportunities for meaning.

- **Avoid the tyranny of technocracy.** Burnett used to say this, and I thought he meant the data-driven computer freaks and the government people or some combination, with the Pentagon thrown in. I did not realize, and perhaps he didn't, that he was talking about the ninety percent of managers who ignore relationships and become technocrats, putting their energies into managing all the stuff that is easy to measure. The concept of technocracy has less to do with technology than it does with a "technical," versus a human, *attitude* about our jobs. The tyranny comes in its suppression of the human spirit at work.

ℰ **Abandon career planning and income plans.** The most frustrated people I have ever known are those who got out of school with a complete plan about their career progress. The frustrated ones fall into two categories: those who did not get what they planned and those who did get what they planned.

ℰ **Avoid "building" a resume** by taking jobs just because they will look good on the CV. There is far less future in doing things *just to have done them* than in doing things *just for the doing of them*. Nothing matters like having good work to do and reveling in the work itself.

ℰ **Expect the unexpected and be ready to embrace change.** Everybody talks about this subject until we're all sick of hearing about it. I believe the only way to be ready is not to be ready—not to burden ourselves with a mass of contingency plans and quick moves but simply to pay attention, expect the unexpected, and go with it until we find our opportunities in the chaos that change brings. So many businesses, large and small, make the same mistake: They do the right thing for the wrong reason, then they don't realize they've done the right thing because they evaluate it through the wrong prism, the prism of their conditioning or their expectations. The same thing happens when they do the wrong thing for the right reason. In the midst of change and chaos, we must evaluate everything with a fresh eye, abandoning expectations and presumptions.

Confessions of an Accidental Businessman

✑ **Take the work seriously, but don't take ourselves so seriously.** One of the greatest barriers to personal growth is our desire to live up to our own image, our own hype. Corporate executives are just terrible about thinking they have to live up to some manufactured image of themselves. *They end up leading the unexamined life because so many of them fear what they might discover.*

✑ **Do not use short-term solutions for long-term problems.** The most obvious quick-hit solution is often the one that comes back to haunt us.

✑ **Never run away from anything.** Always run *to* something. I gave this advice countless times to people who were unhappy in their work for some reason or another—difficult boss, incompatible co-worker, limited future. Of course there are reasons to leave a job, but often the solution to a better situation is in confronting the problem honestly and head-on rather than just leaving it behind, along with all the good things of the job. In so many cases have I seen the problems melt away when identified and addressed in the light of rational discussion.

So much for theory and technique. I've said it all before, and most of you have heard it all before. I reiterate it only because, as I said above, my message is simple and does not change. I have no choice but to repeat myself and try to do it in ways and with stories that make the same point in different settings.

Concentrate on Human Value

If anything becomes clear, looking back over my business career and surveying the business scene today, it is that Dr. Jonas Salk got it right with his comment that we have "concentrated too much on the dollar value of the human and not enough on the human value of the dollar." Though I am optimistic in the long term about the changes going on in business, whether that involves "empowerment" or building a "learning organization" and so on, I still feel the dominant business evaluation of humans is according to their dollar value. This is what all the talk of "lean and mean" and "restructuring" and "downsizing" is about.

These attitudes are driven of course more by the opinions of financial analysts than by anything else. Listen, I understand the absolute need to make profits and to earn back the cost of capital plus a fair return thus increasing stockholder value. No question. No debate. The question and debate involve the issue of time: how short term and how long term.

If you find yourself in this debate, and if you are in a leadership position, I urge you to take the courageous road (yes, the one far less traveled) and opt for the decisions and actions that emphasize human values.

Believe me, the payoff will come in many ways, and the payoff will be enduring.

Epilogue

And to think I used to believe that all the money in the cash register at my friend Jack Davis' father's drug store was his. Little did I know that May, years ago at the Memphis Cotton Carnival, that my popcorn and cotton candy and thrill rides were being paid from the meager profits of Jack's poor father. Seemed like free money to me.

Of course, I never told my mother we did anything but just look around the midway at the carnival. Although she might not have understood about the profits, she would have understood that it was not my money to spend. And if she was sensitive about anything, it was money.

Mother's favorite restaurant was a little Italian cafeteria called Robilio's. Foods like ravioli and veal scallopini seemed the most exotic tastes on earth to a boy and his mother who both had been raised on fried chicken and pork chops and turnip greens and corn bread and biscuits. The biggest treat in my life came once every few months when we had saved enough money to eat there.

Mother always kept the money a secret so she could surprise me. There would come a Sunday after church when the bus would approach our stop at Lamar Terrace, then when I would reach to pull the bell cord to signal the driver, she'd smile and say, "Don't pull the cord. Let's just stay on the bus a while," and I'd know we were headed for Robilio's.

Currently my favorite restaurant in New York is Le Madre, a wonderful place featuring Tuscan food. As I have sat in those rich and redolent surroundings where the cost of one meal would have funded two years' of Robilio lunches, I have thought many times how good it would have been to fly Mother to New York, squire her around in a limo, take her to the museums and galleries she had only seen in books, then go to a different fine restaurant every evening. By the time I could afford to do that, she could not travel.

Before her death in the mid-seventies, she understood that I had become "successful," but she still fretted that I might not yet be the "Christian gentleman" she insisted was her only ambition for me. When I was forty years old, she still expressed the hope that I was finding the opportunity to witness.

"Remember," she would say, "you owe all this success to God." Still, she was proud of my accomplishments and, as editor of *Better Homes and Gardens*, I found myself scheduled to speak at her ladies' groups whenever I visited.

Well, Mom, let me tell you what I'm doing at age sixty-two; I hope it counts for something. When people ask what I'm up to these days, I tell them all the mechanical stuff: writing, speaking, conducting workshops, consulting, serving on boards. But that doesn't quite say it, yet to say it is to sound too self-important or even self-righteous.

I am not a scholar and have not learned anything about business through scholarship. I am only a latter-day consultant and certainly learned little about leadership through consulting. I am just a businessman, an accidental one to be sure, but a pretty good one nonetheless. I have learned all I know on the job and have tried to put together experiences from every job I've had, from copy boy to jet pilot to senior executive, to try to distinguish the connections between them, to discern the patterns they form, to understand the lessons they teach.

It seems to me enormously important that we realize the cumulative nature of experience and turn it to our understanding. It seems equally important that we realize that it doesn't make a damn how much we know about business if we do not understand that relationships are at the heart of it.

I know that people are crying out for human connection in the workplace, and I know that the more computer technology we employ in the doing of our work, the more intense that cry for human connection will be. The only appropriate response is a human response, and responding to that cry will be the greatest challenge of managers and leaders into the next century.

The subject, of course, is values. I have an ambition in business for the rest of my productive life and it is to continue to work with people like Matt Handbury of Murdoch Magazines in Sydney and Doug Greene of New Hope Communications and Jim Donohew of Champion International and Janet Heim of Xerox and Mike Moody and Tom Hoffman of AT&T and Irv Hockaday of Hallmark and Dwight Tierney of Viacom and Kerm Campbell, formerly of Herman Miller now an entrepreneur, and Jack and Peter Herschend of SDC, Inc., and Carol Johnson of U.S. West and Jim Kennedy and Tim Hughes of Cox Enterprises and Gary Adamson of Unison Marketing and Steve Watermeier of Morrison's Restaurants and Bob Teuffel of Rodale and Karen Doherty of the American Management Association and the many other executives who are deeply concerned with how we manifest our values in the workplace.

In my work with businesspeople, I want to live the values

I hold dear, I want to help others live their values, and in some way—however small—I want to take part in the transformation of business, to help business become a place where, indeed, the emphasis is on the liberation of the human spirit and on the human value of the dollar.

So look, Mom, I'm witnessing.

Index

a young publisher's
perspective of, 16–17
a young worker's perception
of, 11–12
buyouts, leveraged, 212–214

Campbell, Kermit, 36, 237
cancer, in the workplace, 115
career
college experience, 14
effect on family life, 74,
90–91
formula for work and
available time, 186
getting "passed over" for a
top job, 208–210
long vs. short term decisions,
157–158
plans and leadership, 232
careers, in the 60s, 28
Carter, John Mack, 154–158
celebration, work as a, 142–143
Chameleon (Diehl), 107
Champion International, 237
chances, danger and taking,
197–198
change
breaking away from
traditions, 177
impact on ego and success of
new ideas, 181
leadership, 232
promotion and, 184–186
using consensus to implement,
178–179
Chappell, Tom, 36
codes, dress, 28
Coffin, Chuck, 110
Colliers, 78
Commercial Telegraphers Union,
13

communication
changing your vocabulary to
fit the situation, 201–203
conferences as a means of
improving, 178–179
growth vocabulary, 229
management, 207–208
memos vs. personal
confrontation, 80–82
regarding changes, 149
compensation, perks as hidden,
169–170
competition, keeping your eye on
the, 195–196
conditions, overcoming adverse
environmental office,
139–140
conferences
as a celebration of work, 144
to implement change,
178–179
as perks, 167
conflicts
in establishing authority, 181
resignation over unresolved
personal, 154–158
confrontation, using memos to
avoid personal, 80–82
contacts, staying in touch with
ordinary people, 70–71
Cox Communications, 136–137
Cox Enterprises, 237
Cox, Otis, 94–95
Craster, Elizabeth D., 81–83,
120, 142–143
creativity, volunteers, 210–211
Curtis, Hugh, 53–54
customers
cost of ego trips, 130–131
opinion polls and, 153
responding to the needs of,
110

roles, female vs. male employees, 89
romance, in the workplace, 99
Runciman, Max, 202

salaries
approving employee, 79–80
female vs. male, 88
sales, advertising, 105–107
salesmen, legendary, 64
Salk, Jonas, on human values, 233
SDC, Inc., 237
secretaries, the changing role of, 88–89, 96
self-education, business and management fundamentals, 16–18
Seney, Noel "Red"
Death Message, 121–122
fatal illness, 41, 116, 120, 141–142
friend and co-worker, 29, 70, 93
sexual harassment, attitudes, 86–90
Sharkey's Machine (Diehl), 107
Sheehan, Mickey, 108
shortcomings, learning from your, 228–229
signals
problem work situation early warning, 102–103
publishing job problem warning, 130–131
recognizing market changes, 190–191
Silk, Wes, 204
Silver Dollar City, 36
solutions, short term vs. long term, 233
Southern Living, 188

spirituality
relationships, 36–37
of work, 33–43
staff
balancing available resources, 147–153
downsizing New Orleans Magazine, 104–105, 107–108
emotional impact of lay offs on, 107–108
sizing to the workload at Better Homes and Gardens, 132–133, 148–149
Stafford, William, 1
standards
creating quality, 176–179
inner expectations and, 65
personal growth and performance, 62–63
stereotypes
based on genetics or work experience, 113–114
executive lifestyle, xi–xii
management, 181–183
stories, finding the local perspective, 108–110
stress, relieving through fun, 139–140
success
chance and, 229
dual ladders of, 179–181
responsibility for, 236
Successful Farming, 141
Sunset, 188
Suter, G., 220

Tagore, Rabindranath, 42–43
talk, whiskey, 74
Tao Te Ching (Lao-tzu), 35

work *(continued)*
   appearances, 29–30
   a caring environment's impact
     on, 3
   community of, 31, 39–41
   fun at, 135–136
   good, 35
   humanity in the workplace,
     230–231
   jobs as a youth, 33–34
   key to excellent, 63–64
   meaningful, 10
   returning to a former
     employer with a
     promotion, 125–126

   romance at, 99
   self-worth and, 204–205
   significance in our lives, 116
   spirituality of, 33–43
   taking it seriously, 233
   union rules and production,
     12–14

Xerox, 237

Young, Ed, 141

About the Author

James A. Autry is a former Fortune 500 executive, an author of four books, a poet, and a consultant whose work has had a significant influence on leadership thinking. His book, *Love and Profit: The Art of Caring Leadership*, won the prestigious Johnson, Smith & Knisely Award as the book that had the most impact on executive thinking in 1992. He currently holds the Dean Helen LeBaron Hilton chair in Leadership at Iowa State University.

He has written the introductions to several books, and his writings have appeared in many anthologies and magazines. In late 1991, the *Kentucky Poetry Review* published a special James A. Autry issue. He received considerable national attention when he was one of the poets featured on Bill Moyers' special series, "The Power of the Word," on PBS. He is also featured in two videos, "Love and Profit" and "Life & Work," both produced by The Excellence in Training Corporation.

Before taking early retirement in 1991 to pursue his present career, Mr. Autry had a distinguished career at Meredith Corporation, where he was senior vice president and president of its magazine group, a 500-million-dollar operation with over 900 employees. He has also been active in many civic and charitable organizations and educational institutions, and most notably has worked with disability rights groups for 25 years. Other involvements have included his work with the Epilepsy Foundation of America, with the national advisory committee of the White House Conference on Families, and with the Des Moines Symphony. He is a founder of the Des Moines National Poetry Festival.

He fulfilled his military service as a jet-fighter pilot in Europe during the cold war. He holds three honorary degrees and, in 1991, the University of Missouri-Columbia awarded him the Missouri Medal of Honor for Distinguished Service in Journalism.

Mr. Autry, who has two grown sons from a previous marriage, lives in Des Moines, Iowa, with his wife, Sally, and their son, Ronald who, at twelve years old, is the proud uncle of Mr. Autry's two grandsons.

Berrett-Koehler Publishers

ERRETT-KOEHLER is an independent publisher of books, periodicals, and other publications at the leading edge of new thinking and innovative practice on work, business, management, leadership, stewardship, career development, human resources, entrepreneurship, and global sustainability.

Since the company's founding in 1992, we have been committed to supporting the movement toward a more enlightened world of work by publishing books, periodicals, and other publications that help us to integrate our values with our work and work lives, and to create more humane and effective organizations.

We have chosen to focus on the areas of work, business, and organizations, because these are central elements in many people's lives today. Furthermore, the work world is going through tumultuous changes, from the decline of job security to the rise of new structures for organizing people and work. We believe that change is needed at all levels—individual, organizational, community, and global—and our publications address each of these levels.

We seek to create new lenses for understanding organizations, to legitimize topics that people care deeply about but that current business orthodoxy censors or considers secondary to bottom-line concerns, and to uncover new meaning, means, and ends for our work and work lives.

See next page for other books from Berrett-Koehler Publishers

Other leading-edge business books from Berrett-Koehler Publishers

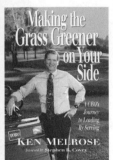

Making the Grass Greener on Your Side
A CEO's Journey to Leading by Serving
Ken Melrose

MAKING THE GRASS GREENER ON YOUR SIDE is the story of how Ken Melrose, CEO of The Toro Company, adopted a philosophy of leading by serving and made it work in a real-world —and often challenging—situation. His mission at Toro has been to build an environment that not only serves the needs of the corporation, but also provides a climate for its constituents—the employees—to grow and develop as human beings. Readers will learn how to cultivate an environment for individual growth and create a win-win situation.

Hardcover, 250 pages, 9/95 • ISBN 1-881052-21-4 CIP • **Item no. 52214-149 $24.95**

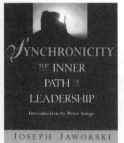

Synchronicity: The Inner Path of Leadership
Joseph Jaworski

SYNCHRONICITY is an inspirational guide to developing the most essential leadership capacity for our time: the ability to collectively shape our future. Joseph Jaworski tells the remarkable story of his journey to an understanding of the deep issues of leadership. It is a personal journey that encourages and enlightens all of us wrestling with the profound changes required in public and institutional leadership, and in our individual lives, for the 21st century. Jaworski offers a new definition of leadership that applies to all types of leaders: community, regional, international, corporate, political.

Hardcover, 228 pages, 6/96 • ISBN 1-881052-94-X CIP • **Item no. 5294X-149 $24.95**

A Higher Standard of Leadership
Lessons from the Life of Gandhi
Keshavan Nair

THIS IS THE FIRST BOOK to apply lessons from Gandhi's life to the practical tasks faced by today's business and political leaders. Through examples from Gandhi's life and writings, Keshavan Nair identifies commitments—to conscience, openness, service, values, and reduced personal attachments—and describes the courage and determination necessary to lead by them. He explores the process of making decisions, setting goals, and implementing actions in the spirit of service that is essential to the realization of a higher standard of leadership in our workplaces and communities.

Hardcover, 174 pages, 10/94 • ISBN 1-881052-58-3 CIP • **Item no. 52583-149 $24.95**

Available at your favorite bookstore, or call 1-800-929-2929

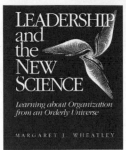
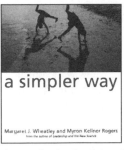

The Courageous Follower
Standing Up To and For Our Leaders
Ira Chaleff

L EADERS CANNOT EXIST without followers. Every great leader must, therefore, be surrounded by great followers. At last, here is a book to balance the hundreds of management books on leadership, which gives followers the insights and tools necessary to partner effectively with their leaders. For anyone who works closely with a leader of any kind, this is a comprehensive guide for positively influencing that relationship and helping the leader use power wisely to accomplish the organization's purpose. It is a handbook that readers can refer to repeatedly when confronted with the challenges of supporting and, at times, correcting a leader.

Hardcover, 280 pages, 6/95 • ISBN 1-881052-66-4 CIP • **Item no. 52664-149 $24.95**

On Our Own Terms
Portraits of Women Business Leaders
Liane Enkelis and Karen Olsen, with Marion Lewenstein
Foreword by Jane Applegate

F IFTEEN WOMEN CEOs and presidents of companies with annual revenues of $10 million or more tell how they got to the top —on their terms. Through personal interviews and striking photographs these business leaders reveal how they broke through the gender barrier to achieve top executive positions, and how they learned to balance family needs with work responsibilities.

Paperback original, 168 pages, 10/95 • ISBN 1-881052-69-9 CIP
Item no. 52699-149 $19.95

Managers As Mentors
Building Partnerships for Learning
Chip R. Bell

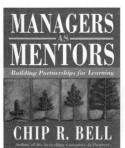

M ANAGERS AS MENTORS is a provocative guide to helping associates grow and adapt in today's tumultuous organizations. Chip Bell persuasively shows that today, mentoring means valuing creativity over control, fostering growth by facilitating learning, and helping others get smart, not just get ahead. His hands-on, down-to-earth advice takes the mystery out of effective mentoring, teaching leaders to be the confident coaches integral to learning organizations.

Hardcover, 206 pages, 6/96 • ISBN 1-881052-92-3 CIP
Item no. 52923-149 $24.95

Available at your favorite bookstore, or call 1-800-929-2929